The Basic Oxford Picture Dictionary

English/Spanish Edition

P9-BIS-933

Margot F. Gramer

Illustrations by

Skip Baker
Graphic Chart & Map Co.
Karen Loccisano
Laura Hartman Maestro
M. Chandler Martylewski
Yoshi Miyake
Joel Snyder

DISCARD

Oxford University Press

Read PC 4629 .G7313 1994
Gramer, Margot
The basic Oxford picture dictionary

Oxford University Press

198 Madison Avenue
New York, NY 10016 USA

Great Clarendon Street
Oxford OX2 6DP England

Oxford New York

Athens Auckland Bangkok Bogotá Buenos Aires Calcutta Cape Town
Chennai Dar es Salaam Delhi Florence Hong Kong Istanbul Karachi
Kuala Lumpur Madrid Melbourne Mexico City Mumbai Nairobi Paris
São Paulo Shanghai Singapore Taipei Tokyo Toronto Warsaw

and associated companies in
Berlin Ibadan

OXFORD AND OXFORD AMERICAN ENGLISH are trademarks of
Oxford University Press.

Library of Congress Cataloging-in-Publication Data

Gramer, Margot.
   (Basic Oxford picture dictionary. Spanish & English)
   The basic Oxford Picture dictionary : English / Spanish / Margot F.
Gramer ; translated by Sergio Gaitán : illustrations by Skip Baker
... (et al.). — English/Spanish ed.
      p.   cm.
   Includes index.
   ISBN 0-19-434571-8
   I. Picture dictionaries, Spanish. 2. Picture dictionaries,
English. 3. Spanish language—Dictionaries—English. 4. English
language—Dictionaries—Spanish. I. Title.
PC4629.G7313 1994
463'.21—dc20   93-41105
                                                 CIP

Copyright © 1994 by Oxford University Press

No unauthorized photocopying.

All rights reserved. No part of this publication may be reproduced,
stored in a retrieval system, or transmitted, in any form or by any means,
electronic, mechanical, photocopying, recording, or otherwise, without
the prior written permission of Oxford University Press.

This book is sold subject to the condition that it shall not, by way of trade
or otherwise, be lent, resold, hired out, or otherwise circulated without
the publisher's prior consent in any form of binding or cover other than
that in which it is published and without a similar condition including this
condition being imposed on the subsequent purchaser.

Illustrations by: Skip Baker, Karen Loccisano, Laura Hartman Maestro,
M. Chandler Martylewski, Yoshi Miyake, Joel Snyder, Graphic Chart &
Map Co.

Icons by Stephan Van Litsenborg

Cover Design by Mark C. Kellogg
Cover Illustration: Karen Loccisano

Printing (last digit): 10 9 8

Printed in China

ACKNOWLEDGMENTS

Oxford University Press gratefully acknowledges the work of the teachers and administrators who helped to shape this book:

Jayme Adelson-Goldstein, Los Angeles Unified School District

Fiona Armstrong, New York City Board of Education

Shirley Brod, Spring Institute for International Education

Ann Creighton, Los Angeles Unified School District

Irene Frankel, The New School for Social Research

Rheta Goldman, North Hollywood Adult Learning Center

Jean Pilger, New York City Board of Education

Norma Shapiro, Los Angeles Unified School District

Renée Weiss, North Hollywood Adult Learning Center

Our special thanks to Jayme Adelson-Goldstein, Fiona Armstrong, and Norma Shapiro, who served as *Dictionary* consultants and authored the accompanying *Teacher's Resource Book*, *Workbook*, and *Picture Cards.* Their commitment to student-centered learning helped guide the development of the *Basic Oxford Picture Dictionary Program.*

El Programa del Basic Oxford Picture Dictionary

El Programa del Basic Oxford Picture Dictionary ha sido desarrollado específicamente para satisfacer las necesidades de estudiantes jóvenes y adultos a nivel principiante, incluyendo a aquéllos con capacidad limitada de leer y escribir. *El Programa del Basic Oxford Picture Dictionary* es en curso flexible para el desarrollo de las cuatro habilidades y satisface las necesidades críticas de principiantes en el estudio de inglés como segunda lengua y como lengua extranjera. La parte central del programa, *El Basic Oxford Picture Dictionary*, proporciona una espléndida presentación visual de vocabulario principal y lenguaje esencial. El *Dictionary*, aún cuando se usa por sí solo, es un recurso de incalculable valor. Sin embargo, cuando el *Dictionary* se usa con todos sus componentes: *Teacher's Resource Book* and *Cassette* (libro de recursos del maestro y cassette), *Workbook* (cuaderno de práctica), *Picture Cards* (juego de tarjetas ilustradas), *Wall Charts* (cartelones), y *Transparencies* (transparencias), forma un programa completo de desarrollo de la lengua que se puede usar con éxito con estudiantes de todas las edades.

El Programa del Basic Oxford Picture Dictionary ofrece tópicos que reflejan las necesidades inmediatas de la lengua y un vocabulario en contexto para desarrollar habilidades esenciales de sobrevivencia. Además, el diseño ordenado es apropiado para el estudiante con capacidad limitada de leer y escribir.

El Basic Oxford Picture Dictionary

El Basic Oxford Picture Dictionary ilustra alrededor de 1,200 palabras y frases de mayor relevancia en las experiencias de jóvenes y adultos principiantes. Las palabras representadas son las de mayor uso por estudiantes que necesitan habilidades básicas en inglés. El vocabulario se presenta con ilustraciones a todo color que retratan cada vocablo en su contexto en la vida real. El *Dictionary* se divide en 12 unidades temáticas: sin embargo, las páginas se pueden usar al azar dependiendo de las necesidades particulares de los estudiantes.

El número limitado de palabras por página y el tipo de letra grande fácil de leer hacen que el *Dictionary* sea más accesible a estudiantes principiantes. La palabra de uso más común se ha escogido para mayor sencillez. (Cuando existen dos vocablos para un objeto, a menudo se incluirán ambos.) Los sustantivos, los adjetivos y las preposiciones son identificados por número, mientras que los verbos se les identifica por letra. Además, las ilustraciones han sido numeradas en orden consecutivo, de izquierda a derecha y de arriba a abajo, dondequiera que fue posible.

Un índice y una guía de pronunciación en el Apéndice ayudan a los estudiantes y los maestros a localizer rápidamente las palabras y su pronunciación correcta. Un juego completo de *Cassettes* ofrece una lectura de todas las palabras en el *Dictionary*.

Usando El Basic Oxford Picture Dictionary Eficazmente

El Basic Oxford Picture Dictionary es un recurso ideal para principiantes y para estudiantes limitados en sus habilidades para leer y escribir. Las sugerencias a continuación están diseñadas para proveer una estructura para el uso eficaz del *Basic Oxford Picture Dictionary* dentro de una lección comunicativa. Para más sugerencias consulte *El Basic Oxford Picture Dictionary Teacher's Resource Book*, el cual contiene una combinación de recursos para maestros y actividades para estudiantes.

1. Seleccione un Tópico que satisfaga las necesidades de sus estudiantes

Los 68 tópicos diferentes que aparecen en las páginas del Contenido del *Dictionary* reflejan las necesidades esenciales de la lengua que tienen los principiantes. Al seleccionar un tópico en particular para enseñar, tome en consideración tanto su plan de clase como las necesidades inmediatas de sus estudiantes. Usted puede envolver a sus estudiantes en el proceso de selección pidiéndoles que escojan del Contenido los tópicos que les interesen. A pesar de que éstos han sido agrupados en 12 unidades temáticas, usted puede recombinar los tópicos en unidades o temas que convengan a cada grupo en particular. Por ejemplo, tal vez usted prefiera combinar ''De compras en el supermercado'' (de la unidad El mercado) con ''La lavandería automática'' (de la unidad Ropa) y ''La oficina de correos'' (de la unidad La comunidad) para crear el nuevo tema de ''Running Errands'' (Haciendo diligencias).

2. Introduzca el Tópico

Haga que los estudiantes vean alguna página seleccionada del *Dictionary*, o la transparencia o el cartelón correspondiente. Antes de que los estudiantes practiquen diciendo algunas palabras, sería de gran ayuda el relacionar el tópico a las vidas de los estudiantes y así dejar que escuchen las palabras en un contexto ya familiar. Use una o más de las sugerencias a continuación para dar a los estudiantes la oportunidad de escuchar las palabras antes de que practiquen su pronunciación.

- Haga preguntas sobre la ilustración haciendo uso del vocabulario previamente aprendido, tal como, "How many people do you see? Can you name something red in the picture? Do you see something you have in your home? Do you see something you use every day?"

- Narre una historia que se relacione con la ilustración. Por ejemplo, para "Describiendo ropa" p. 52–53, hable sobre unos pantalones que usted compró y que le quedaron grandes.

- Traiga ejemplos de objetos que aparecen en la página y pregunte a los estudiantes si los tienen en sus casas, cuánto cuestan, un buen sitio donde comprarlos, y cuándo y cómo se usan.

3. Presente las palabras de la página

Los estudiantes necesitarán escuchar las palabras en más de un contexto para poderlas dominar. El hacer preguntas específicas es una buena forma de presentar el vocabulario en muchos y variados contextos.

- Haga que los estudiantes cubran las palabras al pie de página y haga preguntas que puedan ser contestadas con "Yes," "No," o "Not sure." Por ejemplo, en la lección de "Sentimientos," p. 18–19, pregunte: "Is the man in number 14 close to home? Is he sad? Is he homesick? When you live at home, are you homesick? When you move to another country, can you be homesick?"

- Para presentar los verbos de acción, como per ejemplo los de la lección "Una fiesta de cumpleaños," p. 17, presente los verbos actuándolos. Después de hacerlo cuatro o cinco veces, haga que los estudiantes los actúen con usted. Por último, haga que los estudiantes hagan las acciones mientras usted dice los verbos.

- Describa simplemente cada palabra y haga que los estudiantes la identifiquen diciendo o escribiendo el número de la palabra. Por ejemplo, para la lección de "Joyas y accesorios," p. 55, describa cada pieza de joyería. "It's on my wrist. I tell time with it. It's silver and black. What number word is it?"

4. Verifique la comprensión

Usted puede asegurar el éxito de sus actividades de práctica cuando evalúa en primer lugar la comprensión de sus estudiantes del nuevo vocabulario. Algunas actividades sencillas le ayudarán a hacer tal evaluación.

- Diga las palabras y haga que los estudiantes señalen la ilustración. Visite cada grupo alrededor del salón de clase para ver qué tan bien hacen la actividad los estudiantes.

- Presente un problema y haga que los estudiantes señalen la ilustración que dé la solución. Por ejemplo, para el tópico "Dinero," p. 10, diga: "I have to make a telephone call. What do I need?"

- Seleccione tarjetas ilustradas apropiadas de la colección de *Picture Cards* del *Basic Oxford Picture Dictionary* y haga tarjetas con palabras que correspondan a las ilustraciones. Distribuya las tarjetas con ilustraciones y aquéllas con palabras a diferentes estudiantes y haga que encuentren a la persona que tenga la tarjeta correspondiente. Visite cada grupo en el salón de clase y verifique el progreso de los estudiantes.

- Cubra las palabras al pie de página. Use las tarjetas de "Yes," "No," y "Not sure" del *Teacher's Resource Book* o papeles de diferentes colores y haga que los estudiantes respondan a preguntas de Yes/No levantando su respuesta.

5. Proporcione práctica dirigida

Una vez que los estudiantes comprenden el significado del vocabulario nuevo, es importante proveerles con oportunidades para que trabajen con la pronunciación y el lenguaje nuevo por medio de actividades de práctica controlada.

- Identifique a varios estudiantes líderes para que digan a grupos de sus compañeros las palabras de alguna página seleccionada en el *Dictionary*. Entonces los estudiantes dentro de cada grupo señalarán las ilustraciones apropiadas. Esta actividad refina la pronunciación de los estudiantes y refuerza el vocabulario nuevo.

- Antes de clase, escriba en el pizarrón varias palabras y oraciones con el vocabulario indicado como objetivo. Oculte esto de alguna forma. Haga que los estudiantes se sienten en pares de frente uno a otro, asegurando que la mitad de los estudiantes se sienten viendo el pizarrón y la otra mitad con la espalda hacia el pizarrón. Los estudiantes que ven el pizarrón podrán dictar las palabras u oraciones de los objetivos y luego verificar la exactitud de sus compañeros.

- Haga que en grupos pequeños los estudiantes usen las *Picture Cards* del *Dictionary* para indicar sustituciones de vocabulario nuevo en los ejercicios

de práctica. (Vea en *The Picture Cards Activity Booklet* más sugerencias para práctica dirigida.)

- Haga que los estudiantes trabajen en las actividades más guiadas en las páginas correspondientes del *Basic Oxford Picture Dictionary Workbook*.

- Para dar práctica en escuchar el vocabulario en contexto, use las actividades enfocadas de comprensión auditiva encontradas en *El Basic Oxford Picture Dictionary Teacher's Resource Book*. Más de 30 de estas diferentes actividades ayudan a los estudiantes a reconocer el vocabulario nuevo como parte de diálogos que usan una velocidad, una entonación y acentos normales.

6. Proporcione práctica comunicativa

Las actividades de práctica comunicativa permiten a los estudiantes tomar elementos de la lengua previamente aprendidos y aplicarlos a situaciones nuevas. La práctica comunicativa les da a los estudiantes la oportunidad de ser independientes en un ambiente seguro. *El Basic Oxford Picture Dictionary Teacher's Resource Book* es una fuente excelente de actividades comunicativas. Estas actividades, basadas en los tópicos del *Dictionary*, están diseñadas para mejorar las habilidades de escuchar, hablar, leer, escribir y de participación entre los estudiantes. Los tipos de actividades para escuchar y hablar incluyen:

Total Physical Response Sequences (Secuencias con el método Respuesta Física Total): Los estudiantes trabajan en pares o grupos pequeños para dar y responder a mandatos basados en páginas específicas del *Dictionary*.

Information Exchanges (Intercambios de información): Los estudiantes trabajan en pares para intercambiar información sobre recetas de cocina, pronósticos del tiempo, anuncios publicitarios, etc.

Mixers (Actividades de asociación social): Los estudiantes buscan a compañeros que puedan contestar sus preguntas específicas.

Interviews (Entrevistas): Los estudiantes trabajan en pares para hacer y contestar preguntas y luego apuntar las respuestas de sus compañeros.

Board Games (Juegos de mesa): Grupos de cuatro estudiantes se turnan en preguntar y contestar conforme se mueven las fichas en un juego de mesa.

Language Experience Projects (Proyectos de experiencias con el lenguaje): Los estudiantes trabajan en grupos o con la clase entera para crear diferentes proyectos y luego escribir sobre sus experiencias.

7. Proporcione práctica de lectura y escritura

- Las actividades de lectura y escritura del *Basic Oxford Picture Dictionary Workbook* refuerzan el nuevo vocabulario además de presentarlo en nuevos contextos en unos ejercicios breves de lectura y escritura.

- *El Basic Oxford Picture Dictionary Teacher's Resource Book* tiene tres tipos diferentes de actividades de lectura para cada unidad del *Dictionary*.

Narrative readings (Lecturas narrativas): Los estudiantes hacen predicciones acerca de una ilustración, leen un cuento y responden a unas preguntas de comprensión.

Life skill readings (Lecturas de la vida real): Los estudiantes analizan formularios, tarjetas y letreros auténticos para información específica.

Language Experience Pictures (Ilustraciones describiendo experiencia con el idioma): La clase se desarrolla a través del proceso de crear, dictar, revisar, copiar, y finalmente leer cuentos basados en ilustraciones.

8. Identifique una actividad para implementación práctica

Uno de los mejores regalos que usted les puede dar a sus estudiantes es la oportunidad de usar el lenguaje nuevo y poner a prueba sus habilidades de comunicación en el mundo fuera del salón de clase. Actividades prácticas son la ''tarea'' del salón de clase de inglés como segunda lengua y como lengua extranjera. El identificar este tipo de actividad para sus estudiantes ayuda a relacionar el aprendizaje del lenguaje que ocurrió en el salón de clase con el lenguaje del mundo real.

- Pida a los estudiantes que entrevisten a un miembro de su familia o a un amigo haciendo uso de preguntas que incorporen el vocabulario nuevo. (Las hojas de Interview y de Mixer que se encuentran en el *Teacher's Resource Book* son útiles para estas actividades.)

- Haga que los estudiantes vean revistas, las páginas amarillas de la guía telefónica, tele guías, etc. para identificar ilustraciones o palabras que reflejen el tópico discutido en clase.

- Asigne como tarea las actividades prácticas marcadas con un asterisco en *El Basic Oxford Picture Dictionary Workbook* y luego discuta las respuestas en clase al día siguiente.

CONTENTS

CONTENIDO

Page   Página

I. **Everyday Language**   Lenguaje del diario   2–10

A Classroom   Un salón de clase · · · · · · · · · · · · · · · · · 2
Time: Months and Seasons   El tiempo: meses y estaciones del año · · · · 4
Time: A Calendar   El tiempo: un calendario · · · · · · · · · · · 5
Time: Times of Day   El tiempo: horas del día · · · · · · · · · · 6
Time: The Clock   El tiempo: el reloj · · · · · · · · · · · · · 7
Weather   El clima · 8
Shapes and Colors   Formas y colores · · · · · · · · · · · 9
Money   Dinero · 10

2. **People**   Gente   11–15

People   Gente · 11
Describing People   Describiendo a gente · · · · · · · · · · 12
Daily Routines   Rutinas diarias · · · · · · · · · · · · · · 14

3. **Family**   Familia   16–21

Family   Familia · 16
A Birthday Party   Una fiesta de cumpleaños · · · · · · · · · 17
Feelings   Sentimientos · · · · · · · · · · · · · · · · · 18
Life Events   Eventos de la vida · · · · · · · · · · · · · · 20

4. **The Home**   La casa   22–33

Houses and Surroundings   Casas y sus alrededores · · · · · · 22
An Apartment Building   Un edificio de apartamentos · · · · · 23
A Living Room   Una sala · · · · · · · · · · · · · · · · · 24
A Kitchen   Una cocina · · · · · · · · · · · · · · · · · 25
A Bedroom   Un cuarto de dormir · · · · · · · · · · · 26
A Bathroom   Un baño · · · · · · · · · · · · · · · · · · 27
Housework   Quehaceres domésticos · · · · · · · · · · 28
Cleaning Implements   Utensilios de limpieza · · · · · · · 30
Tools for the Home   Herramientas para el hogar · · · · · · 31
Household Problems   Problemas caseros · · · · · · · · · · 32

CONTENTS (continued)
CONTENDIO (continuación)

5. The Market   El mercado
34–41

Vegetables   Vegetales · · · · · · · · · · · · · · · · · · · 34
Fruits   Frutas · 35
Meat and Seafood   Carnes y mariscos · · · · · · · · · · · · 36
Packaging   Envases · 37
Dairy Products and Other Foods   Productos lácteos y otros alimentos · · · · · · · · 38
Shopping at the Supermarket   De compras en el supermercado · · · · · · · · · 40

6. Meal Time   La hora de comer
42–47

A Table Setting   Una mesa puesta · · · · · · · · · · · · · · · 42
At a Restaurant   En un restaurante · · · · · · · · · · · · · · 43
Common Prepared Foods   Alimentos preparados comunes · · · · · · · · 44
Cooking a Meal   Preparando una comida · · · · · · · · · · · · 46

7. Clothes   Ropa
48–57

Basic Clothes   Ropa básica · · · · · · · · · · · · · · · · · 48
Casual Clothes   Ropa informal · · · · · · · · · · · · · · · · 49
Cold Weather Clothes   Ropa para clima frío · · · · · · · · · · · · 50
Underwear and Sleepwear   Ropa interior y de dormir · · · · · · · · · 51
Describing Clothes   Describiendo ropa · · · · · · · · · · · · · · 52
At the Store (Prepositions I)   En la tienda (Preposiciones I) · · · · · · · · 54
Jewelry and Accessories   Joyas y accesorios · · · · · · · · · · · · 55
Taking Care of Clothes: The Laundromat   Cuidado de la ropa: la lavandería automática · · · 56
Taking Care of Clothes: The Tailor/Dry Cleaner   Cuidado de la ropa: el sastre/el tintorero · · 57

8. Health   La salud
58–67

The Body   El cuerpo · · · · · · · · · · · · · · · · · · · 58
The Face and the Head   La cara y la cabeza · · · · · · · · · · · · 60
Toiletries   Artículos de tocador · · · · · · · · · · · · · · · 61
Aches, Pains, and Injuries   Dolores y heridas · · · · · · · · · · · · 62
Treatments   Tratamientos · · · · · · · · · · · · · · · · · 64
First Aid and Health Care Items   Primeros auxilios y artículos para el cuidado de la salud · · 65
At a Medical Office   En un consultorio médico · · · · · · · · · · · · 66

9. The Community   La comunidad   68–75

The Community   La comunidad · · · · · · · · · · · · · · · 68
Banking   Transacciones bancarias · · · · · · · · · · · · · 70
The Post Office   La oficina de correos · · · · · · · · · · · 71
An Intersection   Una intersección · · · · · · · · · · · · · 72
Emergencies and Natural Disasters   Emergencias y desastres naturales · · · · · · · 74

10. Transportation   Transporte   76–81

Transportation   Transporte · · · · · · · · · · · · · · · · 76
Parts of a Car   Partes de un automóvil · · · · · · · · · · · 77
On the Road (Prepositions II)   En la carretera (Preposiciones II) · · · · · · · 78
At an Airport   En un aeropuerto · · · · · · · · · · · · · · 80

11. Work   Trabajo   82–91

Occupations and Workplaces I   Ocupaciones y lugares de trabajo I · · · · · · · 82
Occupations II   Ocupaciones II · · · · · · · · · · · · · · 84
Occupations III   Ocupaciones III · · · · · · · · · · · · · 86
A Construction Site   Una área de construcción · · · · · · · 87
At Work   En el trabajo · · · · · · · · · · · · · · · · · 88
A Day-Care Center   Una guardería infantil · · · · · · · · · 90

12. Recreation   Recreo   92–95

Leisure   Tiempo libre · · · · · · · · · · · · · · · · · · 92
Celebrate the Holidays   Celebre los días de fiesta · · · · · · · 94

Appendix   Apéndice   96–102

A. Maps   Mapas · 96
B. Numbers   Números · · · · · · · · · · · · · · · · · 100
C. Weights and Measures   Pesos y medidas · · · · · · · · · 101
D. Temperature Conversions   Conversión de temperaturas · · · · · 102

Index   Indice   103–134

English   Inglés · 103
Spanish   Español · · · · · · · · · · · · · · · · · · · 121

pizarra/pizarrón	1. (chalk)board
gis/tiza	2. chalk
borrador	3. eraser
maestra	4. teacher
estudiante	5. student
silla	6. chair
escritorio	7. desk

libro	8. book
papel	9. paper
bolígrafo	10. pen
lápiz	11. pencil
cuaderno	12. notebook
computadora	13. computer

escribir	**A.** write	ver la pantalla	**H.** look at the screen
señalar	**B.** point (to)	cerrar la ventana	**I.** close the window
salir	**C.** go out	abrir un cuaderno	**J.** open a notebook
entrar	**D.** come in	levantar la mano	**K.** raise...hand
leer	**E.** read	conversar	**L.** talk
escuchar	**F.** listen	estar sentado	**M.** sit
trabajar con la computadora	**G.** work at the computer	estar parado	**N.** stand

El tiempo: meses y estaciones del año

① January
S	M	T	W	T	F	S
⑬					1	2
3	4	5	6	7	8	9
10	11	12	13	14	15	16
17	18	19	20	21	22	23
24 31	25	26	27	28	29	30

② February
S	M	T	W	T	F	S
	1	2	3	4	5	6
7	8	9	10	11	12	13
14	15	16	17	18	19	20
21	22	23	24	25	26	27
28						

③ March
S	M	T	W	T	F	S
	1	2	3	4	5	6
7	8	9	10	11	12	13
14	15	16	17	18	19	20
21 ⑭	22	23	24	25	26	27
28	29	30	31			

④ April
S	M	T	W	T	F	S
				1	2	3
4	5	6	7	8	9	10
11	12	13	14	15	16	17
18	19	20	21	22	23	24
25	26	27	28	29	30	

⑤ May
S	M	T	W	T	F	S
						1
2	3	4	5	6	7	8
9	10	11	12	13	14	15
16 23	17 24	18	19	20	21	22
30 31	25	26	27	28	29	

⑥ June
S	M	T	W	T	F	S
	1	2	3	4	5	
6	7	8	9	10	11	12
13	14	15	16	17	18	19
20 ⑮	21	22	23	24	25	26
27	28	29	30			

⑦ July
S	M	T	W	T	F	S
				1	2	3
4	5	6	7	8	9	10
11	12	13	14	15	16	17
18	19	20	21	22	23	24
25	26	27	28	29	30	31

⑧ August
S	M	T	W	T	F	S
1	2	3	4	5	6	7
8	9	10	11	12	13	14
15	16	17	18	19	20	21
22	23	24	25	26	27	28
29	30	31				

⑨ September
S	M	T	W	T	F	S
		1	2	3	4	
5	6	7	8	9	10	11
12	13	14	15	16	17	18
19	20	21 ⑯	22	23	24	25
26	27	28	29	30		

⑩ October
S	M	T	W	T	F	S
				1	2	
3	4	5	6	7	8	9
10	11	12	13	14	15	16
17	18	19	20	21	22	23
24 31	25	26	27	28	29	30

⑪ November
S	M	T	W	T	F	S
	1	2	3	4	5	6
7	8	9	10	11	12	13
14	15	16	17	18	19	20
21	22	23	24	25	26	27
28	29	30				

⑫ December
S	M	T	W	T	F	S
			1	2	3	4
5	6	7	8	9	10	11
12	13	14	15	16	17	18
19	20	21	22	23	24	25
26	27	28	29	30	31	

enero	1. January
febrero	2. February
marzo	3. March
abril	4. April
mayo	5. May
junio	6. June
julio	7. July
agosto	8. August
septiembre	9. September
octubre	10. October
noviembre	11. November
diciembre	12. December
invierno	13. winter
primavera	14. spring
verano	15. summer
otoño	16. fall

January

① Sun.	② Mon.	③ Tues.	④ Wed.	⑤ Thurs.	⑥ Fri.	⑦ Sat.
					⑧ 1	⑨ 2
⑩ 3	4	⑪ 5	⑫ (6)	⑬ 7	8	9
10	11	12	13	14	⑭ 15	16
⑮ 17	18	19	20	21	22	23
24 / 31	25	26	27	28	29	30

⑯

JANUARY	FEBRUARY	MARCH	APRIL	MAY	JUNE	JULY	AUGUST	SEPTEMBER	OCTOBER	NOVEMBER	DECEMBER

domingo	**1.** Sunday		segundo	**9.** 2nd	
lunes	**2.** Monday		tercero	**10.** 3rd	
martes	**3.** Tuesday		ayer	**11.** yesterday	
miércoles	**4.** Wednesday		hoy	**12.** today	
jueves	**5.** Thursday		mañana	**13.** tomorrow	
viernes	**6.** Friday		día	**14.** day	
sábado	**7.** Saturday		semana	**15.** week	
primero / 1º	**8.** 1st		año	**16.** year	

El tiempo: horas del día

mañana	**1.** morning		sol	**5.** sun
tarde	**2.** afternoon		luna	**6.** moon
anochecer	**3.** evening		estrellas	**7.** stars
noche	**4.** night			

reloj	1. clock	las diez y quince	5. ten fifteen
mediodía	2. noon	las diez y treinta	6. ten thirty
medianoche	3. midnight	un cuarto para las once	7. ten forty-five
las diez en punto	4. ten o'clock		

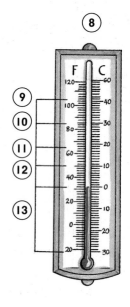

lloviendo	**1.** raining ✓	temperatura	**8.** temperature ✓
nevando	**2.** snowing ✓	caliente	**9.** hot ✓
airoso/ventoso	**3.** windy ✓	cálido	**10.** warm ✓
soleado	**4.** sunny ✓	fresco	**11.** cool ✓
nublado	**5.** cloudy ✓	frío	**12.** cold ✓
cubierto de hielo	**6.** icy ✓	congelación	**13.** freezing ✓
con neblina	**7.** foggy ✗ ✓		

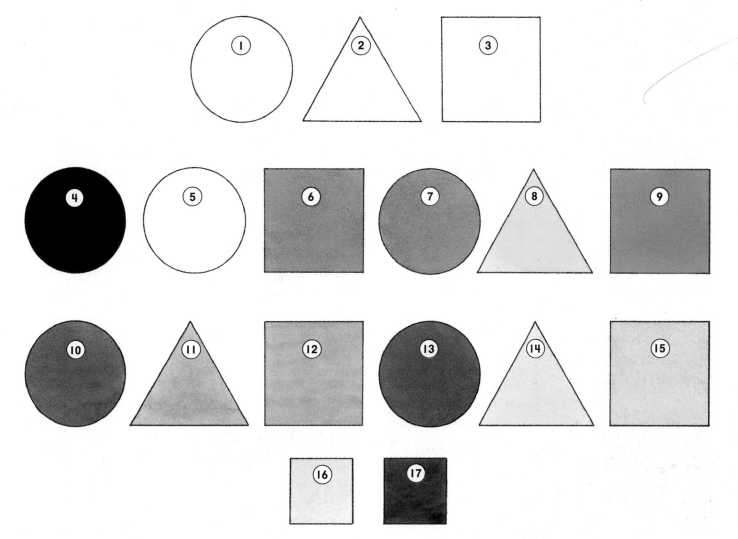

círculo	**1.** circle ✓		café	**10.** brown ✓
triángulo	**2.** triangle ✓		gris	**11.** gray ✓
cuadrado	**3.** square ✓		anaranjado	**12.** orange ✓
negro	**4.** black ✓		morado	**13.** purple ✓
blanco	**5.** white ✓		beige	**14.** beige ✗ ✓
rojo	**6.** red ✓		rosado	**15.** pink ✓
azul	**7.** blue ✓		(azul) claro	**16.** light (blue) ✓
amarillo	**8.** yellow ✓		(azul) oscuro	**17.** dark (blue) ✓
verde	**9.** green ✓			

billetes	**1.** bills		moneda de veinticinco/peseta	**7.** quarter
dólar	**2.** dollar		centavos	**8.** cents
monedas	**3.** coins		cuenta	**9.** check
centavo/chavito prieto	**4.** penny		factura/cuenta	**10.** bill
moneda de cinco/vellón	**5.** nickel		recibo	**11.** receipt
moneda de diez/sencillo	**6.** dime		tarjeta de crédito	**12.** credit card

bebé	**1.** baby	hombre	**5.** man
niña/muchacha	**2.** girl	niño, niña	**6.** child
niño/muchacho	**3.** boy	adolescente	**7.** teenager
mujer	**4.** woman	adulto	**8.** adult

Describiendo a gente

Estatura	Height
alta	**1.** tall
de estatura media	**2.** average height
baja	**3.** short

Peso	Weight
pesado / gordo	**4.** heavy / fat
de peso medio	**5.** average weight
delgado / flaco	**6.** thin / skinny

Tamaño	Size
grande	**7.** big / large
pequeña	**8.** small / little

Pelo/Cabello	Hair		pelo/cabello rubio	**17.** blond hair
barba	**9.** beard		pelo/cabello rojo	**18.** red hair
bigote	**10.** mustache		pelo/cabello café/ castaño	**19.** brown hair
pelo/cabello largo	**11.** long hair			
pelo/cabello corto	**12.** short hair		pelo/cabello negro	**20.** black hair
calvo	**13.** bald		pelo/cabello gris/ canoso	**21.** gray hair
pelo/cabello lacio	**14.** straight hair			
pelo/cabello ondulado	**15.** wavy hair		**Edad**	**Age**
pelo/cabello rizo	**16.** curly hair		joven	**22.** young
			madura	**23.** middle-aged
			anciana	**24.** old

despertarse	**A.** wake up	lavarse la cara	**E.** wash...face
levantarse	**B.** get up	peinarse	**F.** comb...hair
darse una ducha	**C.** take a shower	afeitarse	**G.** shave
cepillarse los dientes	**D.** brush...teeth	vestirse	**H.** get dressed

Daily Routines
Rutinas diarias

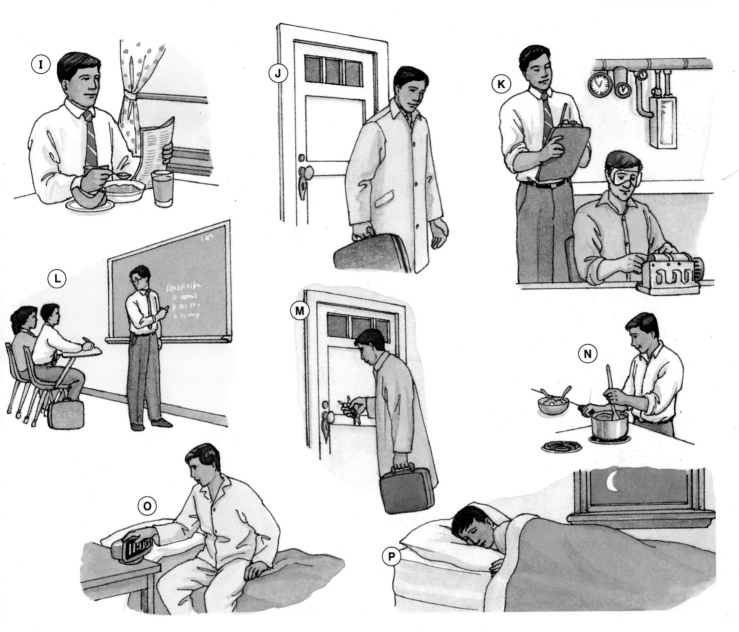

desayunarse	**I.** eat breakfast		regresar a casa	**M.** come home
salir de casa	**J.** leave the house		cocinar la cena	**N.** cook dinner
trabajar	**K.** work		acostarse	**O.** go to bed
estudiar / aprender	**L.** study / learn		dormirse	**P.** go to sleep

abuelos	1. grandparents		esposo	9. husband
padre	2. father		esposa	10. wife
madre	3. mother		padres	11. parents
hermana	4. sister		hijo	12. son
hermano	5. brother		hija	13. daughter
tío	6. uncle		sobrina	14. niece
tía	7. aunt		sobrino	15. nephew
primos	8. cousins			

dar un regalo a	**A.** give a present to		soplar las velitas	**F.** blow out the candles ✓
reír	**B.** laugh		sacar una fotografía	**G.** take a picture
besar	**C.** kiss		beber leche	**H.** drink milk
sonreír	**D.** smile		cortar el pastel / bizcocho	**I.** cut the cake
cantar	**E.** sing		abrir una tarjeta	**J.** open a card

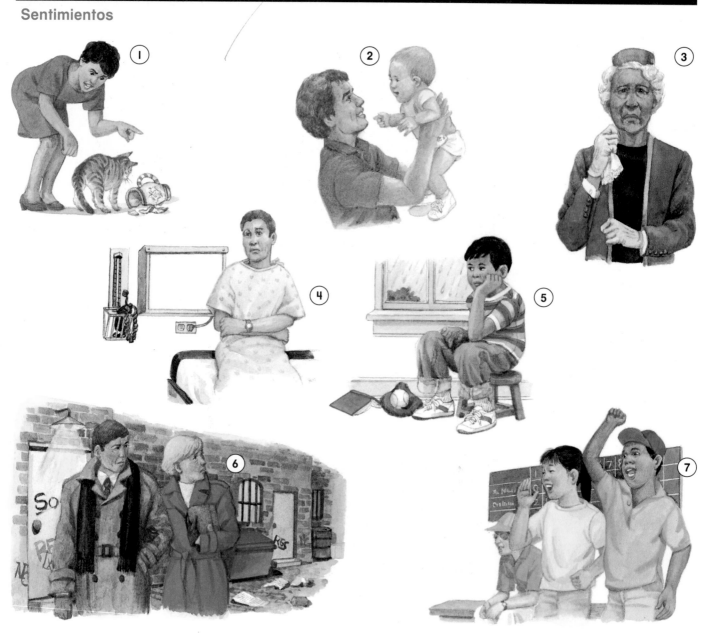

enojado	**1.** angry		aburrido	**5.** bored ✓
feliz/contento	**2.** happy		asustados	**6.** scared
triste	**3.** sad		entusiasmados	**7.** excited ✓
nervioso	**4.** nervous ✓			

sorprendida	**8.** surprised	sediento	**12.** thirsty
preocupada	**9.** worried	avergonzado	**13.** embarrassed
cansado	**10.** tired	melancólico/	**14.** homesick
hambriento	**11.** hungry	nostálgico	

Eventos de la vida

nacer	**A.** be born	conseguir un trabajo	**D.** get a job
empezar la escuela	**B.** start school	retirarse/jubilarse	**E.** retire
graduarse	**C.** graduate		

enamorarse	**F.**	fall in love
casarse	**G.**	get married
divorciarse	**H.**	get divorced
tener un bebé	**I.**	have a baby

mudarse	**J.**	move
enfermarse	**K.**	get sick
morir / fallecer	**L.**	die

Casas y sus alrededores

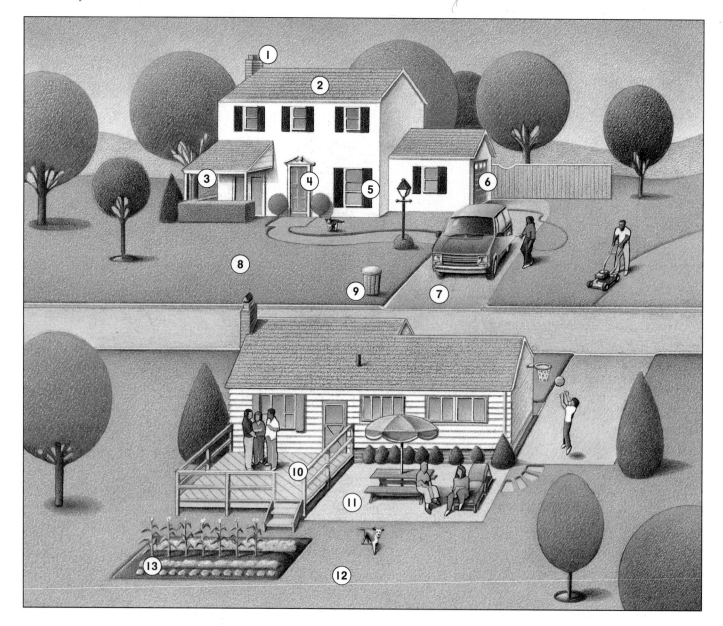

chimenea	**1.** chimney		césped	**8.** lawn
techo	**2.** roof		basurero	**9.** garbage can
porche	**3.** porch		asoleadero	**10.** deck
puerta del frente	**4.** front door		patio	**11.** patio
ventana	**5.** window		patio posterior	**12.** backyard
cochera/garaje	**6.** garage		jardín	**13.** garden
entrada de automóvil	**7.** driveway			

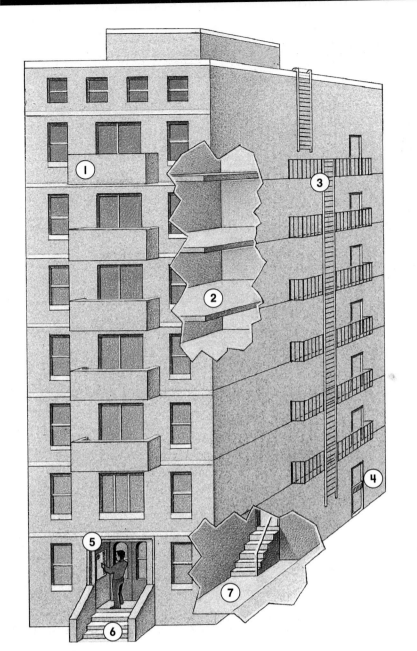

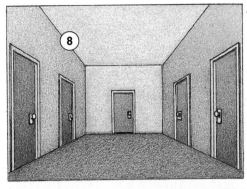

balcón	**1.**	balcony
piso	**2.**	floor
escape de incendio	**3.**	fire escape
salida (de incendio)	**4.**	(fire) exit
entrada	**5.**	entrance
escalones	**6.**	steps
sótano	**7.**	basement

pasillo	**8.**	hall
vestíbulo	**9.**	lobby
ascensor	**10.**	elevator
buzones	**11.**	mailboxes
escalera	**12.**	stairway / stairs
sistema de intercomunicación	**13.**	intercom

techo	**1.** ceiling		mesita	**8.** end table
pared	**2.** wall		mesita central	**9.** coffee table
piso	**3.** floor		alfombra/tapete	**10.** rug
cortinas	**4.** drapes		sofá	**11.** couch/sofa
sillón	**5.** armchair/easy chair		librero/estante	**12.** bookcase
lámpara	**6.** lamp		estéreo	**13.** stereo (system)
teléfono	**7.** (tele)phone		televisión/tele	**14.** television/TV

horno microondas	**1.** microwave (oven)		abrelatas	**9.** can opener
olla / caldero	**2.** pot		fregadero	**10.** kitchen sink
tetera	**3.** (tea)kettle		basurero	**11.** trash can
quemador	**4.** burner		gabinete	**12.** cabinet
sartén	**5.** skillet / (frying) pan		tostadora	**13.** toaster
estufa / hornillo	**6.** stove / range		mostrador	**14.** counter
horno	**7.** oven		congelador	**15.** freezer
asador	**8.** broiler		refrigerador / nevera	**16.** refrigerator

clóset	**1.** closet		almohada	**8.** pillow
cómoda/gavetero	**2.** dresser/bureau		funda	**9.** pillowcase
cajón/gaveta	**3.** drawer		colcha	**10.** bedspread
acondicionador del aire	**4.** air conditioner		cobija	**11.** blanket
cortinas	**5.** curtains		sábanas	**12.** sheets
alfombra	**6.** carpet		reloj despertador	**13.** alarm clock
cama	**7.** bed		mesa de noche	**14.** night table

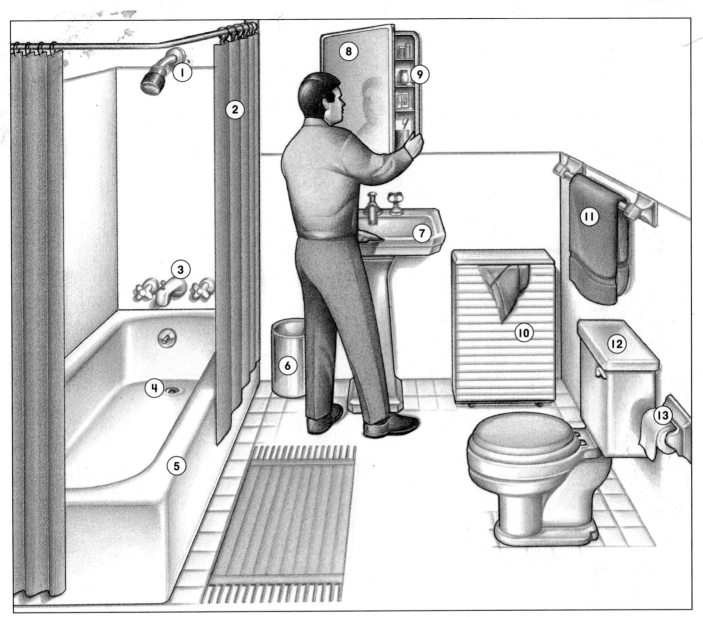

ducha	**1.** shower	espejo	**8.** mirror
cortina de baño	**2.** shower curtain	botiquín	**9.** medicine chest/ medicine cabinet
llave/grifo	**3.** faucet		
desagüe/drenaje	**4.** drain	canasta	**10.** hamper
tina/bañera	**5.** bathtub	toalla	**11.** towel
basurero	**6.** wastebasket	inodoro	**12.** toilet
lavabo	**7.** sink	papel higiénico	**13.** toilet paper

hacer la cama	**A.** make the bed		lavar los platos	**F.** wash the dishes
ordenar el cuarto	**B.** pick up/straighten up the room		secar los platos	**G.** dry the dishes
limpiar el baño	**C.** clean the bathroom		regar las plantas	**H.** water the plants
aspirar la alfombra	**D.** vacuum the rug		rastrillar las hojas	**I.** rake the leaves
sacudir los muebles	**E.** dust the furniture		sacar la basura	**J.** take out the garbage

vaciar el basurero	**K.** empty the wastebasket	limpiar / trapear el piso	**O.** mop the floor
cambiar las sábanas	**L.** change the sheets	lavar la ropa	**P.** do the laundry
barrer el piso	**M.** sweep the floor	plantar un árbol	**Q.** plant a tree
lavar las ventanas	**N.** wash the windows	cortar el césped	**R.** mow the lawn

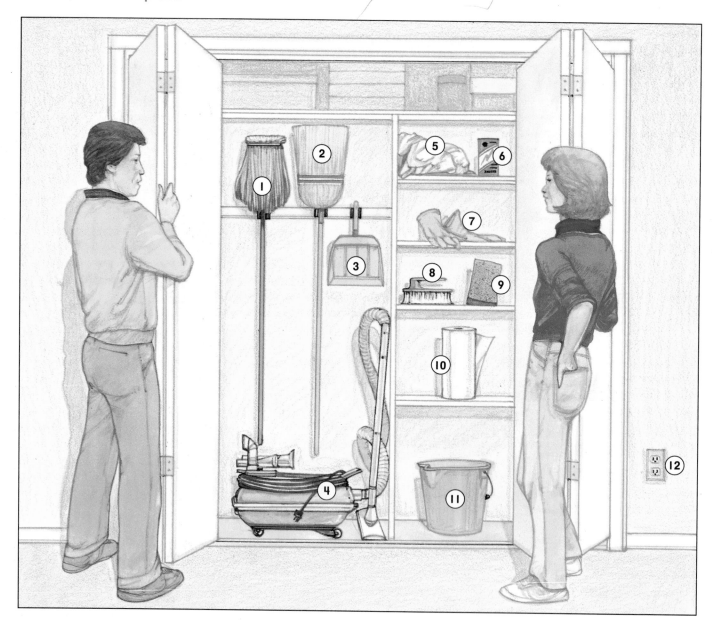

limpiador / trapeador	**1.** mop		guantes de hule	**7.** rubber gloves
escoba	**2.** broom		cepillo	**8.** (scrub) brush
recogedor	**3.** dustpan		esponja	**9.** sponge
aspiradora	**4.** vacuum cleaner		toallas de papel	**10.** paper towels
trapo	**5.** cloth/rag		cubeta	**11.** bucket
limpiador	**6.** cleanser		toma de corriente	**12.** outlet

pinzas	**1.** pliers	caja de herramientas	**9.** toolbox
llave de tuerca	**2.** wrench	escalera	**10.** (step)ladder
destornillador	**3.** screwdriver	manguera	**11.** hose
martillo	**4.** hammer	rastrillo	**12.** rake
serrucho	**5.** saw	pala	**13.** shovel
taladro	**6.** drill	cortadora de césped	**14.** lawn mower
cinta de medir	**7.** tape measure	clavo	**15.** nail
linterna eléctrica	**8.** flashlight	tornillo	**16.** screw

gotera	**1.** leaking roof / ceiling	no hay calefacción	**5.** no heat
pared cuarteada	**2.** cracked wall	inodoro tapado	**6.** stopped-up toilet
ventana rota	**3.** broken window	no hay agua caliente	**7.** no hot water
techo cuarteado	**4.** cracked ceiling	cerradura rota	**8.** broken lock

escalones dañados	**9.** broken steps	cucarachas	**13.** (cock)roaches
llave de agua / grifo con gotera	**10.** dripping faucet	ratones	**14.** mice
desagüe tapado	**11.** clogged drain	sótano inundado	**15.** flooded basement
refrigerador / nevera descompuesto(a)	**12.** refrigerator not working		

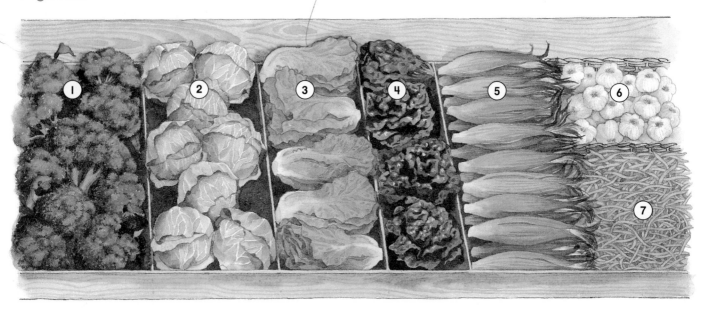

brócoli/brécol	**1.**	broccoli
col/repollo	**2.**	cabbage
lechuga	**3.**	lettuce
espinaca	**4.**	spinach
maíz	**5.**	corn
ajo	**6.**	garlic
habichuelas tiernas/ejotes	**7.**	string beans
tomate	**8.**	tomato

pimiento	**9.**	(bell) pepper
pepino	**10.**	cucumber
papa	**11.**	potato
cebolla	**12.**	onion
zanahoria	**13.**	carrot
hongos	**14.**	mushrooms
chícharos	**15.**	peas

plátanos/guineos	1. bananas	limones verdes	8. limes
uvas	2. grapes	ciruelas	9. plums
manzanas	3. apples	duraznos/ melocotones	10. peaches
naranjas	4. oranges		
peras	5. pears	fresas	11. strawberries
toronjas	6. grapefruit	cerezas	12. cherries
limones	7. lemons	sandías	13. watermelons
		nueces	14. nuts

Carnes y mariscos

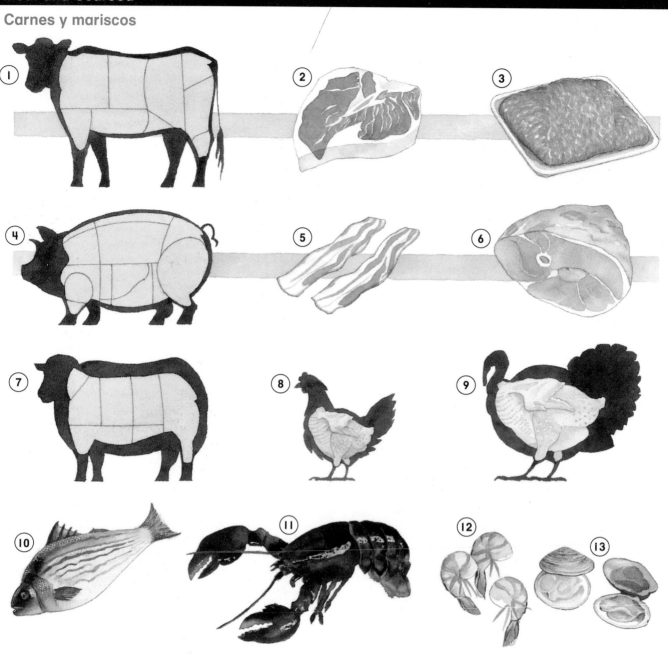

carne de res	**1.** beef		pollo	**8.** chicken
biftec/bistec	**2.** steak		pavo	**9.** turkey
carne molida	**3.** ground meat		pescado	**10.** fish
cerdo/carne de puerco	**4.** pork		langosta	**11.** lobster
tocino	**5.** bacon		camarones	**12.** shrimp
jamón	**6.** ham		almejas	**13.** clams
cordero	**7.** lamb			

un cartón de leche	**1.** a carton of milk
un recipiente de yogur	**2.** a container of yogurt
una botella de soda	**3.** a bottle of soda
un paquete de galletas	**4.** a package of cookies
un paquete de pan	**5.** a loaf of bread
una bolsa de harina	**6.** a bag of flour
un frasco de café	**7.** a jar of coffee
una lata de sopa	**8.** a can of soup
un rollo de papel higiénico	**9.** a roll of toilet paper
una caja de cereal	**10.** a box of cereal
una barra de jabón	**11.** a bar of soap
un tubo de pasta dental	**12.** a tube of toothpaste

Dairy Products and Other Foods

Productos lácteos y otros alimentos

leche	**1.** milk	yogur	**8.** yogurt
crema	**2.** cream	pan	**9.** bread
azúcar	**3.** sugar	cereal	**10.** cereal
huevos	**4.** eggs	café	**11.** coffee
queso	**5.** cheese	té	**12.** tea
mantequilla	**6.** butter	harina	**13.** flour
margarina	**7.** margarine	aceite	**14.** oil

arroz	**15.** rice		galletas	**21.** cookies
frijoles/habichuelas	**16.** (dried) beans		sal	**22.** salt
pasta/fideos	**17.** pasta/noodles		pimienta	**23.** pepper
sopa	**18.** soup		mostaza	**24.** mustard
soda/refresco	**19.** soda/pop		salsa de tomate	**25.** ketchup
jugo	**20.** juice		mayonesa	**26.** mayonnaise

De compras en el supermercado

anaquel/estante	**1.** shelf	báscula/balanza	**7.** scale
pasillo	**2.** aisle	caja registradora	**8.** cash register
canasta de compras	**3.** shopping basket	mostrador de pago	**9.** checkout (counter)
carrito de compras	**4.** shopping cart	abarrotes/víveres	**10.** groceries
cliente	**5.** customer	bolsa	**11.** bag
cajera	**6.** checker/checkout person	empacador	**12.** packer/bagger
		regreso de botellas	**13.** bottle return

empujar	**A.**	push	poner/meter	**E.**	put in
llevar/cargar	**B.**	carry	sacar	**F.**	take out
pagar	**C.**	pay for	pesar	**G.**	weigh
escoger	**D.**	choose/pick out	empacar	**H.**	pack

A Table Setting

Una mesa puesta

mesa	**1.** table		platillo	**8.** saucer
cubiertos	**2.** silverware		salero y pimentero	**9.** salt and pepper shakers
mantelito individual	**3.** place mat		servilleta	**10.** napkin
tazón/plato hondo	**4.** bowl		tenedor	**11.** fork
plato	**5.** plate		cuchillo	**12.** knife
vaso	**6.** glass		cuchara	**13.** spoon
taza	**7.** cup			

cocinero	1. cook	mesera/camarera	7. waitress
lavaplatos	2. dishwasher	menú	8. menu
casilla/caseta	3. booth	silla alta	9. high chair
agua	4. water	sección de fumar	10. smoking section
limpiamesas	5. busboy	sección de no fumar	11. no smoking section
mesero/camarero	6. waiter	cajera	12. cashier

Common Prepared Foods

Alimentos preparados comunes

huevos revueltos	**1.** scrambled eggs
salchicha	**2.** sausage
huevos fritos / estrellados	**3.** fried eggs
pan tostado	**4.** toast
panecillo / panecillo inglés	**5.** muffin / English muffin
wafles	**6.** waffles
panqueques	**7.** pancakes

jarabe / almíbar	**8.** syrup
donas	**9.** donuts
emparedado	**10.** sandwich
hamburguesa	**11.** hamburger
papas fritas	**12.** french fries
perro caliente	**13.** hot dog

Dinner

Dessert

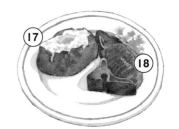

ensalada	**14.** salad	puré de papas	**19.** mashed potatoes
espaguetis	**15.** spaghetti	pollo frito	**20.** fried chicken
piza	**16.** pizza	helado	**21.** ice cream
papa al horno	**17.** baked potato	pastel de manzana	**22.** apple pie
chuleta de puerco	**18.** pork chop		

Preparando una comida

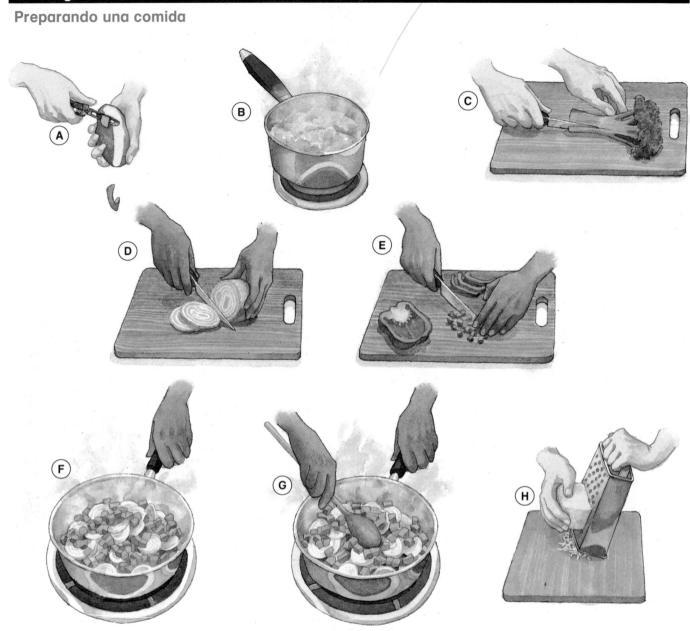

pelar papas	**A.** peel potatoes	picar pimientos	**E.** chop peppers
hervir agua	**B.** boil water	freír cebollas y pimientos	**F.** fry onions and peppers
cortar brócoli/brécol	**C.** cut broccoli	menear cebollas y pimientos	**G.** stir onions and peppers
rebanar cebollas	**D.** slice onions	rallar queso	**H.** grate cheese

cocer vegetales al vapor	**I.** steam vegetables	hornear un guiso	**L.** bake a casserole
vaciar leche	**J.** pour milk	asar pescado	**M.** broil fish
mezclar ingredientes	**K.** mix ingredients		

vestido	**1.** dress		pantalones	**7.** pants
blusa	**2.** blouse		zapato	**8.** shoe
falda	**3.** skirt		traje	**9.** suit
camisa	**4.** shirt		gorra	**10.** cap
corbata	**5.** tie		uniforme	**11.** uniform
cinturón	**6.** belt			

traje de baño (de hombre)	**1.** swimtrunks/bathing suit	gorra de béisbol	**6.** baseball cap
traje de baño (de mujer)	**2.** swimsuit/bathing suit	camiseta	**7.** T-shirt
anteojos/gafas de sol	**3.** sunglasses	zapatos de tenis	**8.** sneakers/athletic shoes
jeans	**4.** jeans	pantalón corto	**9.** shorts
sandalias	**5.** sandals	sudadera/traje de entrenamiento	**10.** warm-up suit

chamarra/chaqueta	1.	jacket		
chaleco (de plumón)	2.	(down) vest		
suéter	3.	sweater		
gorra	4.	hat		
sudadera	5.	sweatshirt		
mochila	6.	backpack		
botas	7.	boots		
impermeable	8.	raincoat		
paraguas	9.	umbrella		
bufanda	10.	scarf		
abrigo	11.	coat		
mitones	12.	mittens		
guantes	13.	gloves		
orejeras	14.	earmuffs		

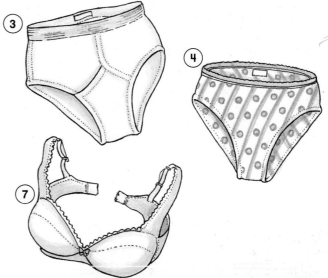

camiseta	**1.** undershirt		sostén	**7.** bra
calzoncillos	**2.** boxer shorts		calcetines	**8.** socks
trusa	**3.** underpants		bata de noche	**9.** nightgown
pantaleta	**4.** panties		pijama	**10.** pajamas
pantimedia	**5.** pantyhose		bata de baño	**11.** bathrobe
medias	**6.** stockings		pantuflas	**12.** slippers

gruesa	**1.** heavy	sucia	**6.** dirty
ligera	**2.** light	alto	**7.** high
nueva	**3.** new	bajo	**8.** low
vieja	**4.** old	angosta	**9.** narrow
limpia	**5.** clean	ancha	**10.** wide

mojado	**11.** wet		suelta	**16.** loose
seco	**12.** dry		pequeña	**17.** small
larga	**13.** long		mediana	**18.** medium
corta	**14.** short		grande	**19.** large
apretada	**15.** tight		extra grande	**20.** extra-large

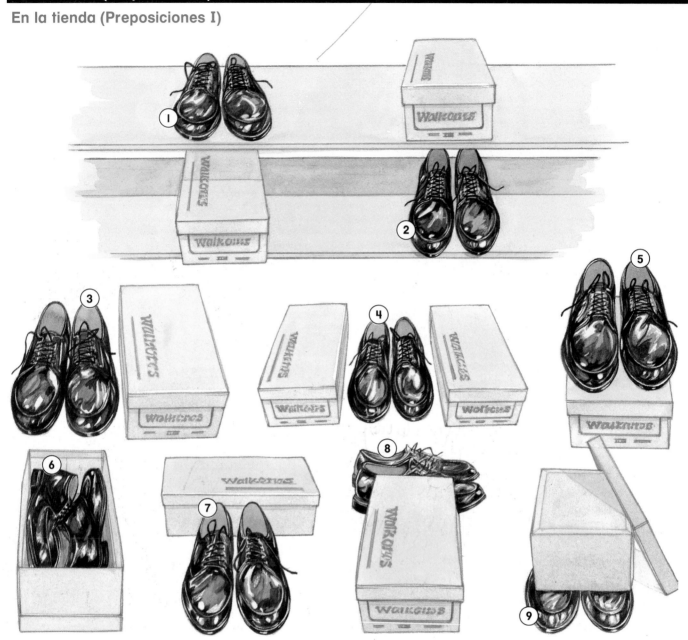

por encima de la caja	**1.** above the box
por debajo de la caja	**2.** below the box
junto a la caja	**3.** next to the box
entre las cajas	**4.** between the boxes
sobre la caja	**5.** on the box
dentro de la caja	**6.** in the box
frente a la caja	**7.** in front of the box
detrás de la caja	**8.** behind the box
debajo de la caja	**9.** under the box

anillo	**1.** ring		reloj	**6.** watch
pulsera	**2.** bracelet		cambio	**7.** change
aretes	**3.** earrings		lentes/anteojos/gafas	**8.** glasses
collar	**4.** necklace		cartera/billetera	**9.** wallet
bolsa	**5.** purse/bag		tarjeta de identificación	**10.** ID card

Cuidado de la ropa: la lavandería automática

lavadora	1. washer / washing machine	poner / meter	A. load / put in
detergente	2. detergent	sacar	B. unload / take out
secadora	3. dryer	planchar	C. iron
ranura	4. slot	doblar	D. fold
canasta de lavandería	5. laundry basket		
tabla de planchar	6. ironing board		
plancha	7. iron		

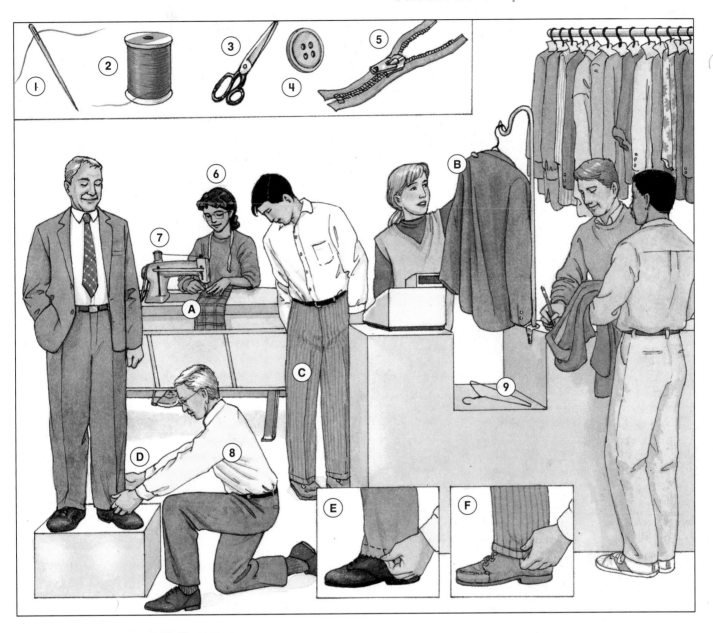

aguja	**1.** needle		coser	**A.** sew	
hilo	**2.** thread		colgar	**B.** hang up	
tijeras	**3.** scissors		probarse	**C.** try on	
botón	**4.** button		corregir/hacer arreglos	**D.** alter/do alterations	
cierre	**5.** zipper				
costurera	**6.** seamstress		alargar	**E.** lengthen	
máquina de coser	**7.** sewing machine		acortar	**F.** shorten	
sastre	**8.** tailor				
gancho	**9.** hanger				

cara	**1.** face		dedo	**8.** finger
cuello	**2.** neck		pulgar	**9.** thumb
hombro	**3.** shoulder		muñeca	**10.** wrist
pecho	**4.** chest		cabeza	**11.** head
mano	**5.** hand		brazo	**12.** arm
cintura	**6.** waist		seno	**13.** breast
cadera	**7.** hip		pierna	**14.** leg

espalda	**15.** back	talón	**22.** heel
muslo	**16.** thigh	dedo del pie	**23.** toe
codo	**17.** elbow	cerebro	**24.** brain
rodilla	**18.** knee	pulmón	**25.** lung
pantorrilla	**19.** calf	corazón	**26.** heart
tobillo	**20.** ankle	estómago	**27.** stomach
pie	**21.** foot		

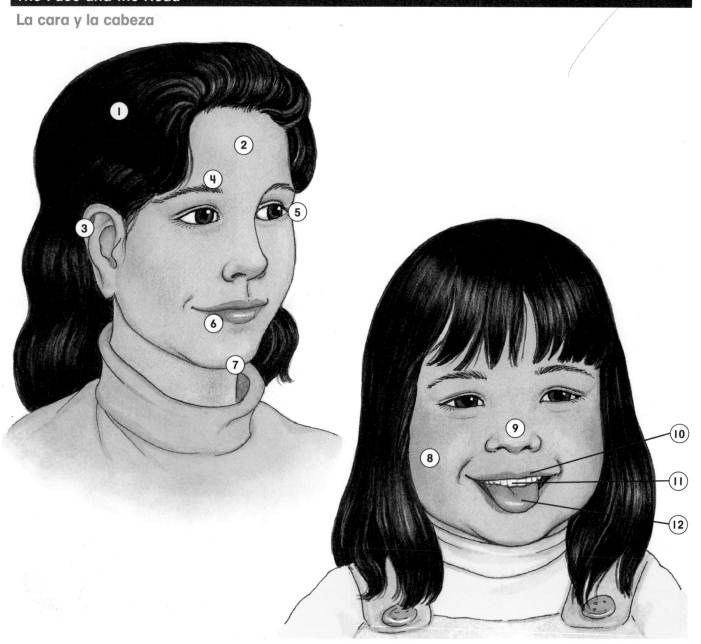

cabello/pelo	**1.** hair		mentón	**7.** chin
frente	**2.** forehead		mejilla	**8.** cheek
oreja	**3.** ear		nariz	**9.** nose
ceja	**4.** eyebrow		labio	**10.** lip
ojo	**5.** eye		diente	**11.** tooth
boca	**6.** mouth		lengua	**12.** tongue

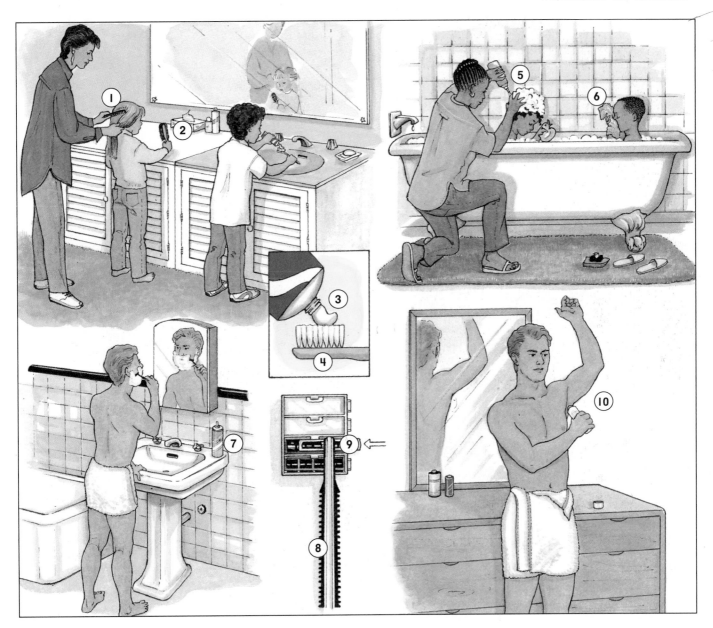

peine	**1.** comb		paño para lavarse	**6.** washcloth
cepillo	**2.** brush		crema de afeitar	**7.** shaving cream
pasta de dientes	**3.** toothpaste		navaja de afeitar	**8.** razor
cepillo de dientes	**4.** toothbrush		hojas de afeitar	**9.** blades
champú	**5.** shampoo		desodorante	**10.** deodorant

resfriado	**1.** cold		dolor de oído	**7.** earache
fiebre	**2.** fever		cortadura	**8.** cut
dolor de cabeza	**3.** headache		contusión	**9.** bruise
dolor de espalda	**4.** backache		sarpullido	**10.** rash
dolor de estómago	**5.** stomachache		picadura de insecto	**11.** insect bite
dolor de diente/muela	**6.** toothache			

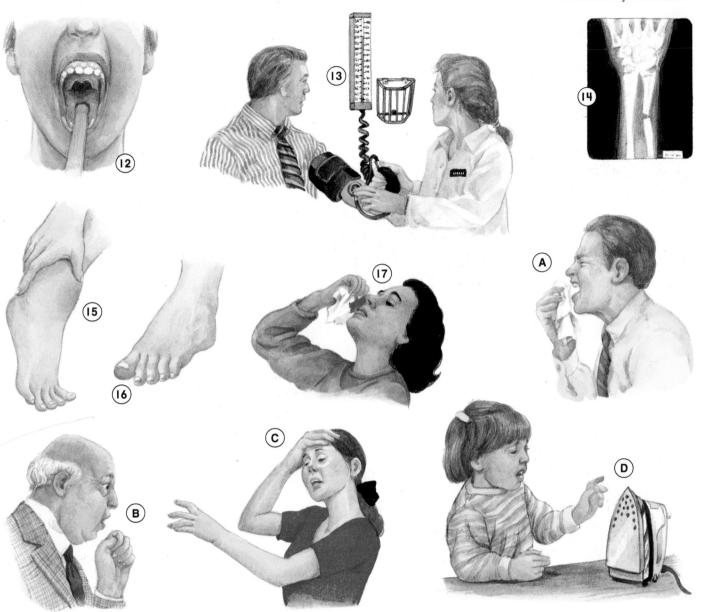

dolor de garganta	12. sore throat	estornudar	A. sneeze
alta presión	13. high blood pressure	toser	B. cough
brazo roto	14. broken arm	desmayarse	C. faint
tobillo hinchado	15. swollen ankle	quemarse	D. burn...self
dedo del pie infectado	16. infected toe		
nariz sangrienta	17. bloody nose		

Treatments

Tratamientos

tener una operación	**A.** have an operation
descansar	**B.** get rest
tener puntos	**C.** get stitches
tomar medicina	**D.** take medicine
ser enyesado	**E.** get a cast
hacer ejercicio	**F.** exercise
ponerse a dieta	**G.** go on a diet

medicinas/drogas	**I.** medicine/drugs
píldoras	**2.** pills
crema/ungüento	**3.** cream/ointment
inyección	**4.** injection/shot
gotas	**5.** drops
gotero	**6.** medicine dropper
atomizador	**7.** spray

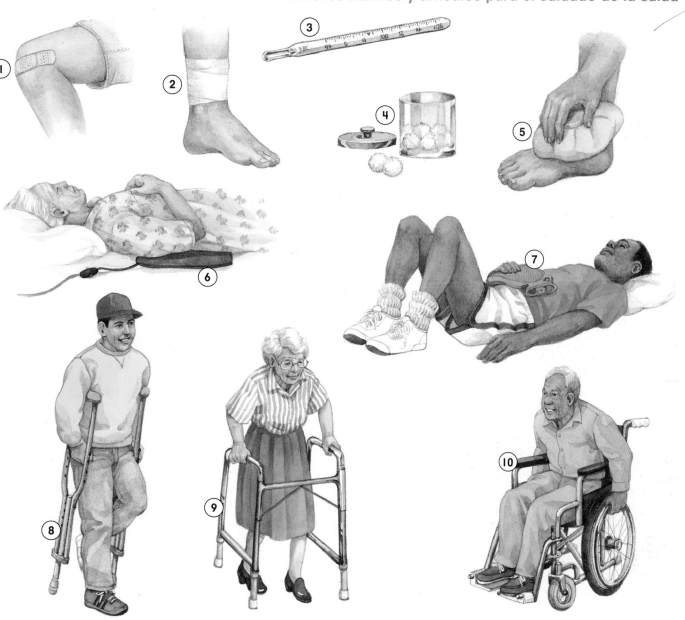

curita	1. Band-Aid	toalla calentadora	6. heating pad
vendaje	2. bandage	bolsa de agua caliente	7. hot water bottle
termómetro	3. thermometer	muletas	8. crutches
bolitas de algodón	4. cotton balls	andador	9. walker
compresa de hielo	5. ice pack	silla de ruedas	10. wheelchair

sala de espera	**1.** waiting room	médico	**6.** doctor
recepcionista	**2.** receptionist	enfermera	**7.** nurse
formulario de seguro	**3.** insurance form	sala de reconocimiento	**8.** examining room
tarjeta de seguro	**4.** insurance card	rayos equis	**9.** X ray
paciente	**5.** patient	receta	**10.** prescription

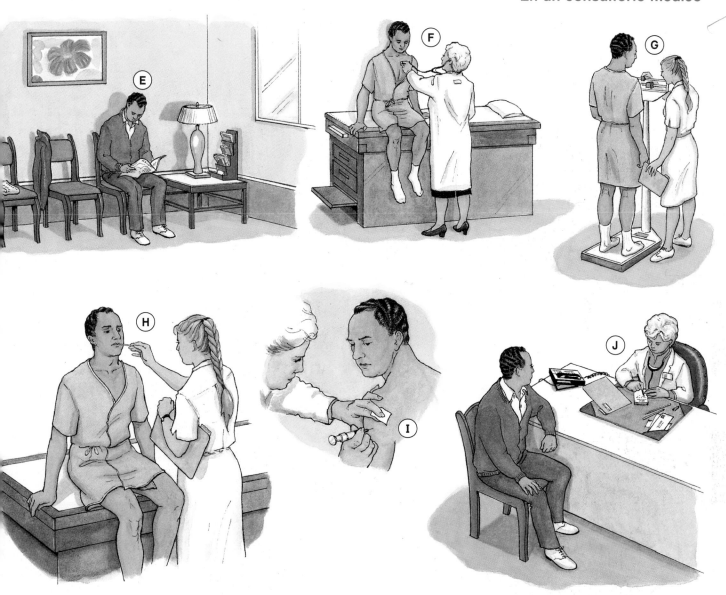

llenar el formulario	**A.** fill out the form	examinar al paciente	**F.** examine the patient
escribir el nombre en letra de molde	**B.** print name	pesar al paciente	**G.** weigh the patient
		tomar la temperatura	**H.** take...temperature
firmar el nombre	**C.** sign name	poner una inyección	**I.** give a shot / an injection
demostrar la tarjeta de seguro	**D.** show insurance card		
esperar	**E.** wait	escribir una receta	**J.** write a prescription

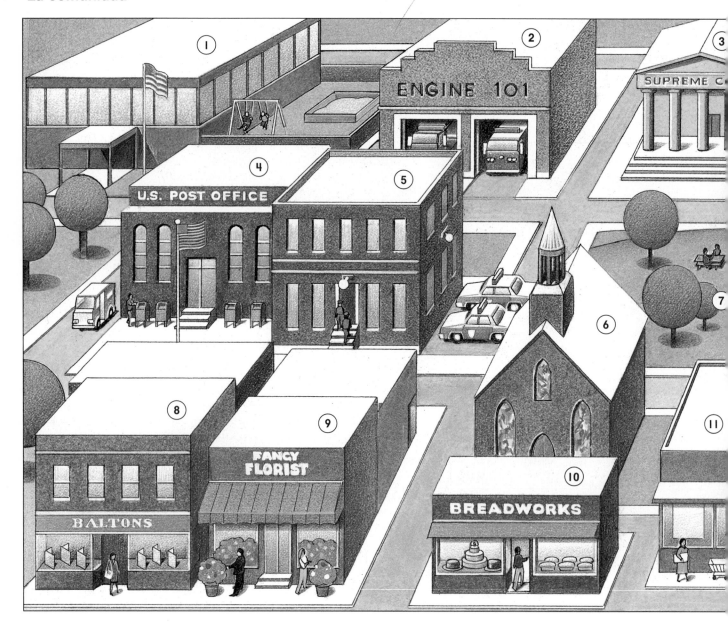

escuela	**1.** school	iglesia	**6.** church
estación de bomberos	**2.** firehouse	parque	**7.** park
palacio de justicia	**3.** courthouse	librería	**8.** bookstore
oficina de correos	**4.** post office	florería	**9.** florist
estación de policía/ comisaría	**5.** police station	panadería	**10.** bakery
		supermercado	**11.** supermarket

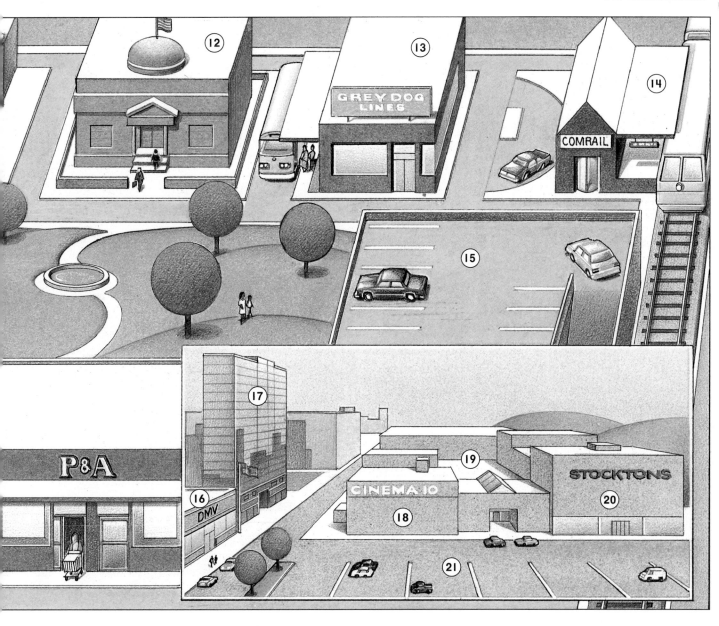

ayuntamiento	**12.** city hall	edificio de oficinas	**17.** office building
estación de autobuses	**13.** bus station	cine	**18.** movie theater
estación de trenes	**14.** train station	galería	**19.** mall
estacionamiento	**15.** parking garage	tienda por departamentos	**20.** department store
Departamento de Registro de Vehículos	**16.** Department of Motor Vehicles (DMV)	estacionamiento / aparcamiento	**21.** parking lot

Transacciones bancarias

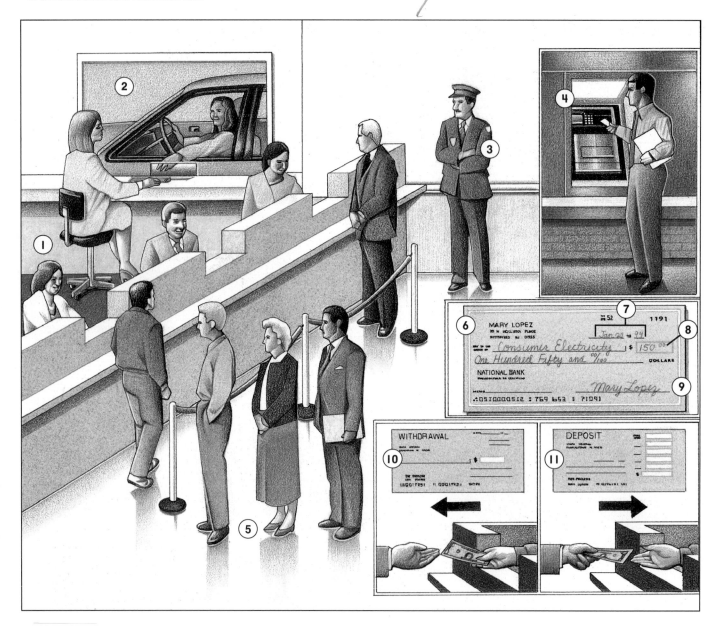

pagadora	**1.** teller	fecha	**7.** date
ventana de servicio rápido	**2.** drive-thru window	cantidad	**8.** amount
guardia de seguridad	**3.** security guard	firma	**9.** signature
pagador automático	**4.** ATM/cash machine	comprobante de retiro	**10.** withdrawal slip
cola	**5.** line	comprobante de depósito	**11.** deposit slip
cheque	**6.** check		

caerse	**A.** fall (down)		envenenarse	**D.** swallow poison
tener un ataque al corazón	**B.** have a heart attack		sofocarse	**E.** choke
ahogarse	**C.** drown			

Transporte

automóvil	**1.** car		tren subterráneo	**7.** subway	
autobús	**2.** bus		avión	**8.** plane	
camión	**3.** truck		tren	**9.** train	
camioneta	**4.** van		barco	**10.** ship	
motocicleta	**5.** motorcycle		bicicleta	**11.** bicycle	
taxi	**6.** taxi(cab)/cab				

placa / chapa de matrícula	**1.** license plate
faros delanteros	**2.** headlights
batería	**3.** battery
capó	**4.** hood
parabrisas	**5.** windshield
maletera / baúl	**6.** trunk
tanque de gasolina	**7.** gas tank
llanta	**8.** tire

tablero	**9.** dashboard
volante	**10.** steering wheel
encendido	**11.** ignition
freno	**12.** brake
acelerador	**13.** accelerator / gas pedal
cinturón de seguridad	**14.** seat belt
asiento para niño	**15.** car seat

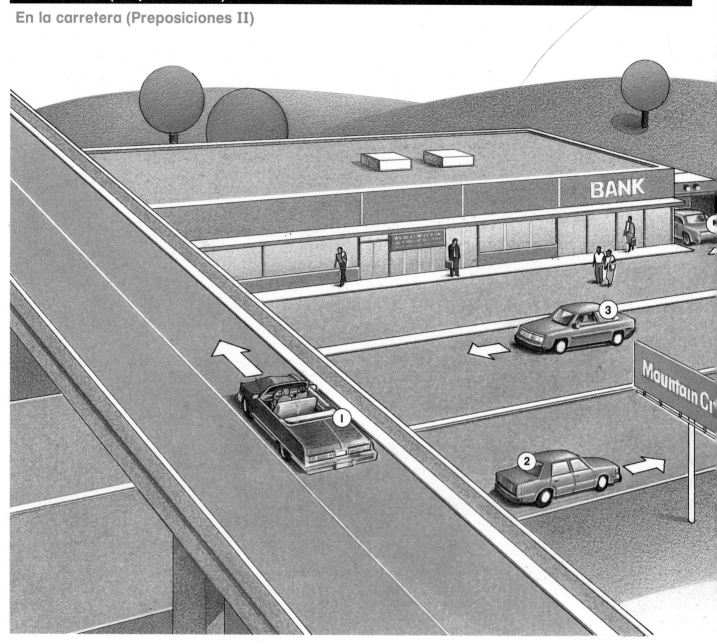

sobre la carretera	**1.** over the highway	de / desde la ciudad	**3.** from / away from the city
a / hacia la ciudad	**2.** to / toward the city	a través del banco	**4.** through the bank

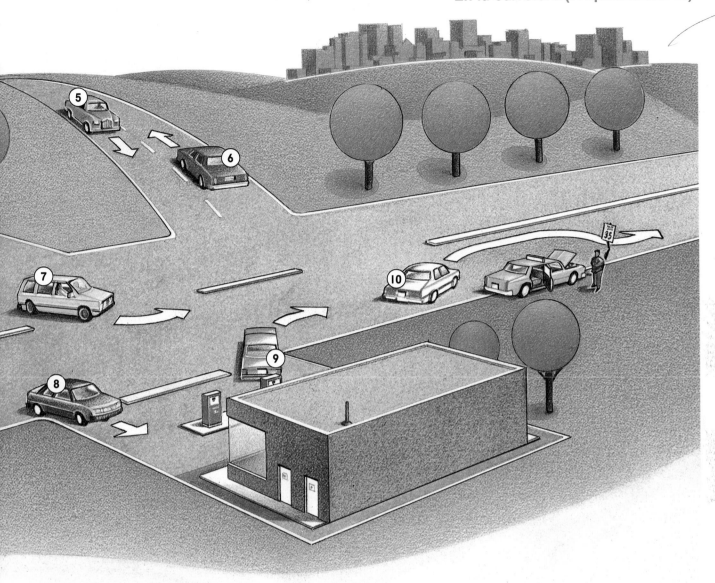

bajando la colina	**5.** down the hill	entrando a la gasolinera	**8.** into the gas station
subiendo la colina	**6.** up the hill	saliendo de la gasolinera	**9.** out of the gas station
cruzando el tráfico	**7.** across the traffic	alrededor del accidente	**10.** around the accident

pasajero	**1.** passenger
boleto	**2.** ticket
maleta/equipaje	**3.** suitcase/luggage
control de seguridad	**4.** security check
tarjeta de embarque/pasabordo	**5.** boarding pass

puerta/salida	**6.** gate
auxiliar de vuelo	**7.** flight attendant
piloto	**8.** pilot
reclamo de equipaje	**9.** baggage claim

obrero de fábrica	**13.** factory worker	camionero	**19.** truck driver
capataz	**14.** foreman	granjero	**20.** farmer
chofer / conductor de autobús	**15.** bus driver	soldado	**21.** soldier
carpintero	**16.** carpenter	operaria de máquina de coser	**22.** sewing machine operator
empleado de mantenimiento	**17.** maintenance man	operador de tren	**23.** (train) conductor
pescador	**18.** fisherman		

Ocupaciones III

secretaria	**1.** secretary	contadora	**9.** accountant
mecanógrafo	**2.** typist / word processor	abogado	**10.** lawyer
archivista	**3.** file clerk	vendedor	**11.** salesperson
programadora	**4.** computer programmer	niñera	**12.** babysitter
mensajero	**5.** messenger	bailarina / bailarín	**13.** dancer
fotógrafo	**6.** photographer	cantante	**14.** singer
reportera	**7.** reporter	actor / actriz	**15.** actor / actress
hombre / mujer de negocios	**8.** businessman / businesswoman	artista	**16.** artist

traer/dejar	**A.** bring/drop off		tomar una siesta	**G.** take a nap
cambiar pañales	**B.** change diapers		mecer	**H.** rock
jugar	**C.** play		tomar en los brazos	**I.** hold
gatear	**D.** crawl		llorar	**J.** cry
correr	**E.** run		recoger/levantar	**K.** pick up
alimentar	**F.** feed		vestir	**L.** dress

Actividades al aire libre	Outdoor Activities	Deportes	Sports
acampar / ir de campamento	**A.** go camping	jugar tenis	**C.** play tennis
		jugar fútbol americano	**D.** play football
hacer excursión	**B.** go hiking	jugar baloncesto	**E.** play basketball
		jugar fútbol	**F.** play soccer
		jugar béisbol	**G.** play baseball
		ir a esquiar	**H.** go skiing

Actividades bajo techo	Indoor Activities		Ejercicio	Exercise	
tocar un instrumento	**I.** play an instrument		ir a nadar	**M.** go swimming	
ir al cine	**J.** go to the movies		ir a correr	**N.** go running	
ver televisión	**K.** watch TV				
escuchar música	**L.** listen to music				

La Nochevieja	**New Year's Eve**	**La Pascua**	**Easter**
beber champaña	**A.** drink champagne	pintar huevos de Pascua	**E.** paint Easter eggs
brindar	**B.** make a toast	ir en busca de huevos de Pascua	**F.** go on an Easter egg hunt
El Día de los Enamorados	**Valentine's Day**		
dar regalos de San Valentín	**C.** give valentines	**El Día de los Soldados Muertos**	**Memorial Day**
recibir flores	**D.** get flowers	flotar una bandera	**G.** wave a flag
		ver un desfile	**H.** watch a parade
		visitar un cementerio	**I.** visit a cemetery

El 4 de julio	**Fourth of July**	El Día de Acción de Gracias	**Thanksgiving**
hacer una parrillada/ comer al aire libre	**J.** have a barbecue/ picnic	reunirse con familia y amigos	**O.** get together with family and friends
ver fuegos artificiales	**K.** watch fireworks	dar gracias	**P.** give thanks
		comer una gran comida	**Q.** eat a big meal
El Día de las Brujas	**Halloween**		
esculpir una calabaza	**L.** carve out a pumpkin		
disfrazarse	**M.** wear a costume	La Navidad	**Christmas**
salir por obsequios o travesuras	**N.** go trick-or-treating	enviar tarjetas	**R.** send cards
		ir de compras navideñas	**S.** go Christmas shopping
		decorar el árbol	**T.** decorate the tree

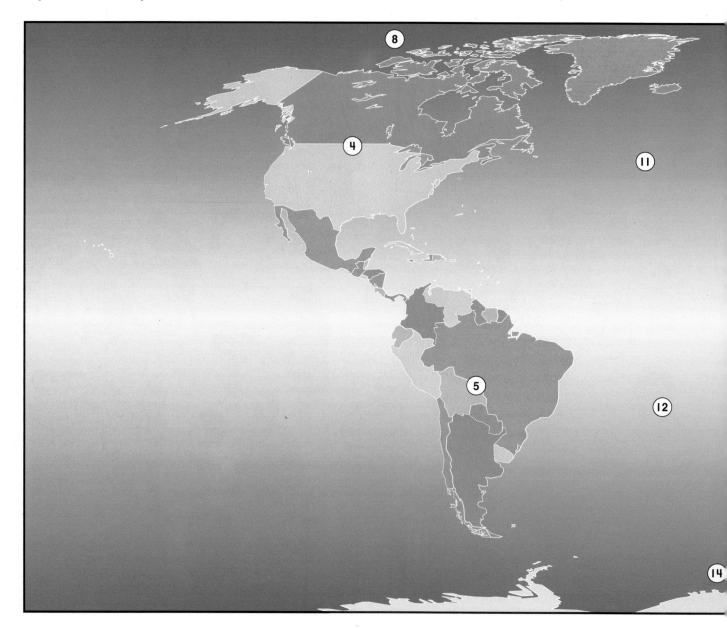

Continentes	Continents	Océanos	Oceans
Asia	**1.** Asia	Artico	**8.** Arctic
Africa	**2.** Africa	Pacífico Norte	**9.** North Pacific
Europa	**3.** Europe	Pacífico Sur	**10.** South Pacific
Norteamérica	**4.** North America	Atlántico Norte	**11.** North Atlantic
Suramérica	**5.** South America	Atlántico Sur	**12.** South Atlantic
Australia	**6.** Australia	Indico	**13.** Indian
Antártica	**7.** Antarctica	Antártico	**14.** Antarctic

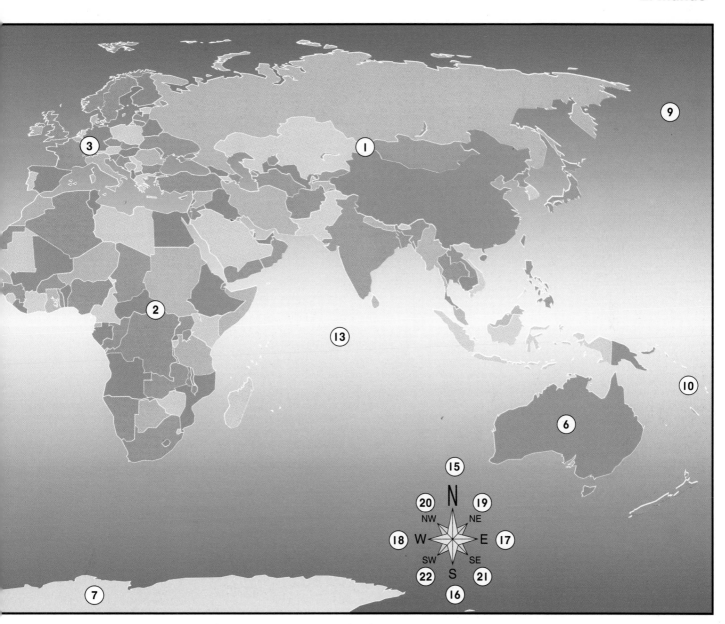

Orientaciones		Directions
norte	**15.**	north
sur	**16.**	south
este	**17.**	east
oeste	**18.**	west
noreste	**19.**	northeast
noroeste	**20.**	northwest
sureste	**21.**	southeast
suroeste	**22.**	southwest

Alabama	**1.** Alabama		Indiana	**14.** Indiana
Alaska	**2.** Alaska		Iowa	**15.** Iowa
Arizona	**3.** Arizona		Kansas	**16.** Kansas
Arkansas	**4.** Arkansas		Kentucky	**17.** Kentucky
California	**5.** California		Luisiana	**18.** Louisiana
Colorado	**6.** Colorado		Maine	**19.** Maine
Connecticut	**7.** Connecticut		Maryland	**20.** Maryland
Delaware	**8.** Delaware		Massachusetts	**21.** Massachusetts
Florida	**9.** Florida		Michigan	**22.** Michigan
Georgia	**10.** Georgia		Minesota	**23.** Minnesota
Hawaii	**11.** Hawaii		Misisipí	**24.** Mississipi
Idaho	**12.** Idaho		Misurí	**25.** Missouri
Illinois	**13.** Illinois		Montana	**26.** Montana

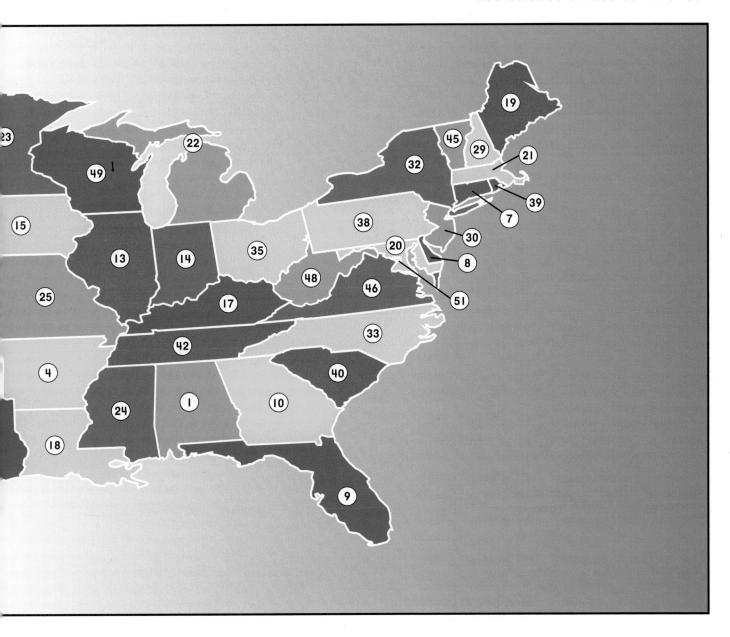

Nebraska	**27.** Nebraska		Carolina del Sur	**40.** South Carolina
Nevada	**28.** Nevada		Dakota del Sur	**41.** South Dakota
New Hampshire	**29.** New Hampshire		Tenesí	**42.** Tennessee
Nueva Jersey	**30.** New Jersey		Texas	**43.** Texas
Nuevo México	**31.** New Mexico		Utah	**44.** Utah
Nueva York	**32.** New York		Vermont	**45.** Vermont
Carolina del Norte	**33.** North Carolina		Virginia	**46.** Virginia
Dakota del Norte	**34.** North Dakota		Washington	**47.** Washington
Ohio	**35.** Ohio		Virginia Occidental	**48.** West Virginia
Oklahoma	**36.** Oklahoma		Wisconsin	**49.** Wisconsin
Oregón	**37.** Oregon		Wyoming	**50.** Wyoming
Pensilvania	**38.** Pennsylvania		Distrito de Columbia	**51.** District of Columbia
Rhode Island	**39.** Rhode Island			

Apéndice B: números

uno	1	one		mil	1,000	a/one thousand
dos	2	two		un millón	1,000,000	a/one million
tres	3	three				
cuatro	4	four				
cinco	5	five		primero	1st	first
seis	6	six		segundo	2nd	second
siete	7	seven		tercero	3rd	third
ocho	8	eight		cuarto	4th	fourth
nueve	9	nine		quinto	5th	fifth
diez	10	ten		sexto	6th	sixth
once	11	eleven		séptimo	7th	seventh
doce	12	twelve		octavo	8th	eighth
trece	13	thirteen		noveno	9th	ninth
catorce	14	fourteen		décimo	10th	tenth
quince	15	fifteen				
dieciséis	16	sixteen				
diecisiete	17	seventeen				
dieciocho	18	eighteen				
diecinueve	19	nineteen				
veinte	20	twenty				
veintiuno	21	twenty-one				
treinta	30	thirty				
cuarenta	40	forty				
cincuenta	50	fifty				
sesenta	60	sixty				
setenta	70	seventy				
ochenta	80	eighty				
noventa	90	ninety				
cien/ciento	100	a/one hundred				
quinientos	500	five hundred				
seiscientos veintiuno	621	six hundred (and) twenty-one				

Abreviaciones	Abbreviations	
onzas	ounces	oz
cucharadita	teaspoon	tsp
cucharada	tablespoon	tbs
pinta	pint	pt
cuarto	quart	qt
galón	gallon	gal
libra(s)	pound(s)	lb(s)
pulgada	inch	in
pie/pies	foot/feet	ft
yarda(s)	yard(s)	yd(s)
milla	mile	mi

litro	liter	l
mililitro	milliliter	ml
gramo	gram	g
miligramo	milligram	mg
kilogramo	kilogram	kg
metro	meter	m
centímetro	centimeter	cm
kilómetro	kilometer	km

Medidas líquidas   **Liquid Measure**

cucharadita   teaspoon   cucharada   tablespoon

taza   cup   un cuarto de taza   a quarter cup

un tercio de taza   a third cup   media taza   a half cup

1 oz	29.6 ml
1 c	236.5 ml
1 pt	473 ml
1 qt	.946 l
1/2 gal	1.893 l
1 gal	3.786 l

1 tbs	3 tsp	1/2 oz
1 c	16 tbs	8 oz
1 pt	2 c	16 oz
1 qt	2 pt	32 oz
1/2 gal	2 qt	64 oz
1 gal	4 qt	128 oz

Longitud, altura y distancia   **Length, Height, and Distance**

regla   ruler

vara de una yarda   yardstick

cinta de medir   measuring tape

1 ft	12 in
1 yd	3 ft
1 mi	1,760 yds

1 in	2.54 cm
1 ft	30.48 cm
1 yd	.941 m
1 mi	1.609 km

Pesos sólidos   **Solid Weights**

1 lb	454 g
1 kg	2.205 lbs

Apéndice D: conversión de temperaturas

Abreviaciones   **Abbreviations**

grados Fahrenheit	degrees Fahrenheit	°F
grados Centígrados	degrees Celsius/Centigrade	°C

From Fahrenheit to Centigrade/Celsius
De Fahrenheit a Centígrados

subtract 32, multiply by 5, divide by 9
reste 32, multiplique por 5, divida entre 9

50°F   50
         -32
          18 x 5 = 90

          90 ÷ 9 = 10°C

From Centigrade/Celsius to Fahrenheit
De Centígrados a Fahrenheit

multiply by 9, divide by 5, add 32
multiplique por 9, divida entre 5, sume 32

10°C   10 x 9 =   90

              90 ÷ 5 =   18
                            +32
                             50°F

Two numbers occur after words in the index: the first refers to the page where the word is illustrated and the second to the item number of the word on that page. For example, above [ə bŭv′] **54**/1 means that the word *above* is the item numbered 1 on page 54. If only a bold number appears, then that word is part of the unit title or a subtitle.

The index includes a pronunciation guide for all the words illustrated in the book. This guide uses symbols commonly found in dictionaries for native speakers. These symbols, unlike those used in transcription systems such as the International Phonetic Alphabet, tend to preserve spelling and so should help you to become more aware of the connections between written English and spoken English.

Consonants

[b] as in **back** [băk]　　[k] as in **kiss** [kĭs]　　[sh] as in **ship** [shĭp]
[ch] as in **cheek** [chēk]　[l] as in **leg** [lĕg]　　[t] as in **tape** [tāp]
[d] as in **date** [dāt]　　[m] as in **man** [măn]　[th] as in **three** [thrē]
[dh] as in **the** [dh]　　[n] as in **neck** [nĕk]　[v] as in **vest** [vĕst]
[f] as in **face** [fās]　　[ng] as in **ring** [rĭng]　[w] as in **waist** [wāst]
[g] as in **gas** [găs]　　[p] as in **pack** [păk]　[y] as in **yard** [yärd]
[h] as in **half** [hăf]　　[r] as in **rake** [rāk]　[z] as in **zip** [zĭp]
[j] as in **jeans** [jēnz]　[s] as in **sad** [săd]　　[zh] as in **measure** [mĕzh′ər]

Vowels

[ā] as in **bake** [bāk]　　[ī] as in **lime** [līm]　　[ōō] as in **cool** [kōōl]
[ă] as in **back** [băk]　　[ĭ] as in **lip** [lĭp]　　[ŏŏ] as in **book** [bŏŏk]
[ä] as in **bar** [bär]　　[ï] as in **heel** [hïl]　　[ow] as in **brown** [brown]
[ē] as in **bean** [bēn]　　[ō] as in **post** [pōst]　[oy] as in **boy** [boy]
[ĕ] as in **bed** [bĕd]　　[ŏ] as in **box** [bŏks]　[ŭ] as in **cut** [kŭt]
[ë] as in **pear** [për]　　[ö] as in **lawn** [lön]　[ü] as in **curb** [kürb]
　　　　　　　　　　　　　　　or **for** [för]　　[ə] as in **above** [ə bŭv′]

All pronunciation symbols used are alphabetical except for the schwa [ə], which is the most frequent vowel sound in English. If you use it appropriately in unstressed syllables, your pronunciation will sound more natural.

You should note that an umlaut ([¨]) calls attention to the special quality of vowels before [r]. (The sound [ö] can also represent a vowel not followed by [r] as in *lawn*.) You should listen carefully to native speakers to discover how these vowels actually sound.

Stress

This guide also follows the system for marking stress used in many dictionaries for native speakers.
　(1)　Stress is not marked if a word consisting of a single syllable occurs in isolation.
　(2)　Where stress is marked, two levels are distinguished:
　　　a bold accent [′] is placed after each syllable with primary stress.
　　　a light accent [′] is placed after each syllable with secondary stress.

Syllable Boundaries

Syllable boundaries are indicated by a single space.

NOTE: The pronunciation used in this index is based on patterns of American English. There has been no attempt to represent all of the varieties of American English. Students should listen to native speakers to hear how the language actually sounds in a particular region.

Index

A

Abbreviations [ə brē'vē ā'shənz]   101
above [ə bŭv']   54/1
accelerator [ăk sĕl'ə rā'tər]   77/13
Accessories [ăk sĕs'ə rēz]   55
accident [ăk'sə dənt]   74/4
accountant [ə kown'tənt]   86/9
Aches [āks]   62–63
across [ə krös']   79/7
Activities, Indoor [ĭn'dör' ăk tĭv'ə tēz]   93
Activities, Outdoor
    [owt'dör' ăk tĭv'ə tēz]   92
actor [ăk'tər]   86/15
actress [ăk'trəs]   86/15
address [ă'drəs]   71/9
address, return [rə türn' ə drĕs']   71/7
adult [ə dŭlt']   11/8
Africa [ă'frĭ kə]   96/2
afternoon [ăf'tər nōōn']   6/2
Age [āj]   13
air conditioner [ër' kən dĭ'shə nər]   26/4
Airport [ër'pört']   80–81
aisle [ī'əl]   40/2
Alabama [ăl'ə bă'mə]   98/1
alarm clock [ə lärm' klŏk']   26/13
Alaska [ə lăs'kə]   98/2
alter [öl'tər]   57/D
alterations [öl'tə rā'shənz]   57/D
ambulance [ăm'byə ləns]   74/5
America, North [nörth' ə mĕr'ə kə]   96/4
America, South [sowth' ə mĕr'ə kə]   96/5
amount [ə mownt']   70/8
angry [ăng'grē]   18/1
ankle [ăng'kəl]   59/20
ankle, swollen [swō'lən ăng'kəl]   63/15
Antarctic Ocean [ănt ärk'tĭk ō'shən]   96/14
Antarctica [ănt ärk'tĭ kə]   96/7
Apartment Building
    [ə pärt'mənt bĭl'dĭng]   23
apartment manager
    [ə pärt'mənt măn'ĭ jər]   84/10
apple pie [ă'pəl pī']   45/22
apples [ă'pəlz]   35/3
appliances, fix [fĭks' ə plī'əns əz]   88/A
appliances, repair [rə për' ə plī'əns əz]   88/A
April [ā'prəl]   4/4
Arctic Ocean [ärk'tĭk ō'shən]   96/8
Arizona [ăr'ə zō'nə]   98/3
Arkansas [är'kən sö']   98/4
arm [ärm]   58/12
arm, broken [brō'kən ärm']   63/14

armchair [ärm'chër']   24/5
around [ə rownd']   79/10
arrive [ə rĭv']   81/D
artist [är'təst]   86/18
Asia [ā'zhə]   96/1
At the store [ăt dhə stör']   54
athletic shoes [ăth lĕ'tĭk shōōz']   49/8
Atlantic Ocean, North
    [nörth' ăt lăn'tĭk ō'shən]   96/11
Atlantic Ocean, South
    [sowth' ăt lăn'tĭk ō'shən]   96/12
ATM machine [ā'tē ĕm' mə shēn']   70/4
attendant [ə tĕn'dənt]   82/4
attendant, flight [flīt' ə tĕn'dənt]   80/7
August [ö'gəst]   4/8
aunt [ănt]   16/7
Australia [ö strāl'yə]   96/6
average height [ăv'rəj hīt']   12/2
average weight [ăv'rəj wāt']   12/5
away from [ə wā' frŭm]   78/3

B

baby [bā'bē]   11/1
baby, have a [hăv' ə bā'bē]   21/1
babysitter [bā'bē sĭt'ər]   86/12
back [băk]   59/15
backache [băk'āk']   62/4
backpack [băk'păk']   50/6
backyard [băk'yärd']   22/12
bacon [bā'kən]   36/5
bag [băg]   40/11, 55/5
bag of flour [băg' əv flow'ər]   37/6
baggage claim [băg'ĭj klām']   80/9
bagger [băg'ər]   40/12
bags, check [chĕk băgz']   81/A
bake a casserole [bāk' ə kăs'ə rōl]   47/L
baked potato [bākt' pə tā'tō]   45/17
bakery [bā'kə rē]   68/10
balcony [băl'kə nē]   23/1
bald [böld]   13/13
bananas [bə nă'nəz]   35/1
bandage [băn'dĭj]   65/2
Ban-Aid [bănd'ād']   65/1
Banking [băng'kĭng]   70
bar of soap [bär' əv sōp']   37/11
barbeque, have a [hăv' ə bär'bə kyōō']   95/J
barber [bär'bər]   82/10
barber shop [bär'bər shŏp']   82/11
baseball, play [plā' bās böl']   92/G
baseball cap [bās' böl kăp']   49/6
basement [bās'mənt]   23/7

basement, flooded [flŭ′əd bās′mənt] 49/6
basket, laundry [lôn′drē băs′kət] 56/5
basket, shopping [shŏp′ ĭng băs′kət] 40/3
basketball, play [plā′ băs′kət böl′] 92/E
bathing suit [bā′dhĭng sōōt′] 49/1–2
bathrobe [băth′rōb′] 51/11
Bathroom [băth′rōōm′] 27
bathroom, clean the
     [klēn dhə băth′rōōm′] 28/C
bathtub [băth′tŭb′] 27/5
battery [băt′ə rē] 77/3
be born [bē′ börn′] 20/A
beans [bēnz] 39/16
beard [bïrd] 13/9
beauty salon [byōō′tē să lŏn′] 82/9
bed [bĕd] 26/7
bed, go to [gō′ tə bĕd′] 15/O
bed, make the [māk′ dhə bĕd′] 28/A
Bedroom [bĕd′rōōm′] 26
bedspread [bĕd′ sprĕd′] 26/10
beef [bēf] 36/1
behind [bə hīnd′] 54/8
beige [bāzh] 9/14
bell pepper [bĕl′ pĕp′ər] 34/9
below [bə lō′] 54/2
belt [bĕlt] 48/6
bench [bĕnch] 72/12
between [bə twēn′] 54/4
bib [bĭb] 90/8
bicycle [bī sī kəl] 76/11
big [bĭg] 12/7
bill [bĭl] 10/11
bills [bĭlz] 10/1
Birthday Party [bürth′dā pär′tē] 17
black [blăk] 9/4
black hair [blăk′ hër′] 13/20
blades [blādz] 61/9
blanket [blăng′kət] 26/11
blond hair [blŏnd′ hër′] 13/17
blood pressure, high [hī blŭd′ prĕsh′ər] 63/13
bloody nose [blŭd′ē nōz′] 63/17
blouse [blows] 48/2
blow out the candles
     [blō′ owt dhə kăn′dəlz] 17/F
blue [blōō] 9/7
blue, dark [därk′ blōō′] 9/17
blue, light [līt′ blōō′] 9/16
board [börd] 2/1
boarding pass [bör′ding păs′] 80/5
Body [bŏ′dē] 58–59
boil water [boyl′ wŏ′tər] 46/B

book [bŏŏk] 2/8
bookcase [bŏŏk′kās′] 24/12
bookstore [bŏŏk′stör′] 68/8
booth [bōōth] 43/3
boots [bōōts] 50/7
bored [börd] 18/5
born, be [bē′ börn′] 20/A
bottle [bŏt′əl] 90/4
bottle, hot water [hŏt wŏ′tər bŏt′əl] 65/7
bottle of soda [bŏt′əl əv sō′də] 37/3
bottle return [bŏt′əl rētürn′] 40/13
bowl [bōl] 42/4
box of cereal [bŏks′əv sïr′ēəl] 37/10
boxer shorts [bŏk′sər shörts] 51/2
boy [boy] 11/3
bra [brŏ] 51/7
bracelet [brās′lət] 55/2
brain [brān] 59/24
brake [brāk] 77/9
bread [brĕd] 38/9
bread, loaf of [lōf′əv brĕd] 37/5
breakfast, eat [ēt′brĕk′fast] 15/I
breast [brĕst] 58/13
bring [brĭng] 91/A
broccoli [brŏk′lē] 34/1
broccoli, cut [kŭt′brŏk′lē] 46/C
broil fish [broyl′fīsh′] 47/M
broiler [broy′lər] 25/8
broken arm [brō′kən ärm′] 63/14
broken lock [brō′kən lŏk′] 32/8
broken steps [brō′kən stĕps′] 33/9
broken window [brō′kən wĭn′dō] 32/3
broom [brōōm] 30/2
brother [brŭdh′ər] 16/5
brown [brown] 9/10
brown hair [brown′ hër′] 13/19
bruise [brōōz] 62/9
brush [brŭsh] 30/8, 61/2
brush . . . teeth [brŭsh′ . . . tēth′] 14/D
bucket [bŭk′ət] 30/11
build furniture [bĭld′für′nə chər] 88/K
build houses [bĭld′how′zəz] 88/J
bureau [byōōr′ō] 26/2
burner [bür′nər] 25/4
burn . . . self [bürn′ . . . sĕlf′] 63/D
bus [bŭs] 76/2
bus, drive a [drīv′ə bŭs′] 89/O
bus, wait for the [wāt′ för dhə bŭs′] 73/K
bus driver [bŭs′drī′vər] 85/15
bus station [bŭs′stā′shən] 69/13
bus stop [bŭs′stŏp′] 72/11

busboy [bŭs′ boy′] 43/5
businessman [bĭz′ nəs măn′] 86/8
businessman [bĭz′ nəs wŏŏm′ ən] 86/8
butcher [bŏŏ′ chər] 82/6
butcher shop [bŏŏ′ chər shŏp′] 82/7
butter [bŭt′ ər] 38/6
button [bŭt′ ən] 57/4
buy groceries [bī′ grō′ sə rēz] 73/G

C

cab [kăb] 76/6
cab, drive a [drīv′ ə kăb′] 89/P
cabbage [kăb′ ĭj] 34/2
cabinet [kăb′ ə nət] 25/12
cabinet, medicine
   [měd′ ə sən kăb′ ə nət] 27/9
cake, cut the [cŭt′ dhə kāk′] 17/I
Calendar [kăl′ ən dər] 5
calf [kăf] 59/19
California [kăl′ ə för′ nyə] 98/5
camping, go [gō′ kăm′ pĭng] 92/A
can of soup [kăn′ əv sōōp′] 37/8
can opener [kăn′ ō′ pə nər] 25/9
candles, blow out the
   [blō′ owt dhə kăn′ dəlz] 17/F
cap [kăp] 48/10
cap, baseball [bās′ böl kăp′] 49/6
car [kär] 76/1
Car, Parts of a [pärts′ əv ə kär′] 77
car seat [kär′ sēt′] 77/15
card, open a [ō′ pən ə kärd′] 17/J
cards, send [sĕnd′ kärdz′] 95/R
carpenter [kär′ pən tər] 85/16
carpet [kär′ pət] 26/6
carrot [kär′ ət] 34/13
carry [kär′·ē] 41/B
cars, fix [fĭks′ kärz′] 88/B
cars, repair [rə pĕr′ kärz′] 88/B
carton of milk [kär′ tən əv mĭlk] 37/1
carve out a pumpkin
   [kärv′ owt′ ə pŭmp′ kən] 95/L
cash machine [kăsh′ mə shēn′] 70/4
cash register [kăsh′ rĕ′ jə stər] 40/8
cashier [kă shĭr′] 43/12
casserole, bake a [bāk′ ə kăs′ ə rōl] 47/L
cast, get a [gĕt′ ə kăst′] 64/E
ceiling [sē′ lĭng] 24/1
ceiling, cracked [krăkt′ sē′ lĭng] 32/4
ceiling, leaking [lē′ kĭng sē′ lĭng] 32/1
Celebrate the Holidays
   [sĕl′ ə brāt dhə hŏl ə dāz] 94–95

cemetery, visit a [vĭz′ ət ə sĕm′ ə tĕr′ē] 94/I
centimeter [sĕn′ tə mē′ tər] 101
cents [sĕnts] 10/8
cereal [sïr′ ē əl] 38/10
cereal, box [bŏks′ əv sïr′ ē əl] 37/10
chair [chĕr] 2/6
chalk [chök] 2/2
chalkboard [chök′ börd′] 2/1
champagne, drink [drĭngk′ shăm pān′] 94/A
change [chānj] 55/7
change diapers [chānj′ dī′ pərz] 91/B
change the sheets [chānj′ dhə shēts′] 29/L
check [chĕk] 10/10, 70/6
check bags [chĕk′ băgz′] 81/A
checker [chĕk′ ər] 40/6
checkout [chĕk′ owt] 40/9
checkout counter [chĕk′ owt kown′ tər] 40/9
checkout person [chĕk′ owt pür′ sən] 40/6
cheek [chēk] 60/8
cheese [chēz] 38/5
cheese, grate [grāt′ chēz′] 46/H
cherries [chĕr′ ēz] 35/12
chest [chĕst] 58/4
chest, medicine [měd′ ə sən chĕst′] 27/9
chicken [chĭk′ ən] 36/8
chicken, fried [frīd′ chĭk′ ən] 45/20
child [chīld] 11/6
child-care worker [chīld′ kĕr′ wür′ kər] 90/1
children, take care of
   [tāk′ kĕr′ əv chĭl′ drən] 89/L
chimney [chĭm′ nē] 22/1
chin [chĭn] 60/7
choke [chōk] 75/E
choose [chōōz] 41/D
chop peppers [chŏp′ pĕp′ ərz] 46/E
Christmas [krĭs′ məs] 95
Christmas shopping, go
   [gō′ krĭs′ məs shŏp′ ĭng] 95/E
church [chürch] 68/6
circle [sür′ kəl] 9/1
city hall [sĭ′ tē höl′] 69/12
clams [klămz] 36/13
Classroom [klăs′ rōōm] 2–3
clean [klēn] 52/5
clean the bathroom
   [klēn′ dhə băth′ rōōm′] 28/C
Cleaning Implements
   [klēn′ ĭng ĭm′ plə mənts] 30
cleanser [klēn′ zər] 30/6
climb [klīm] 87/I
clock [klŏk] 7/1

clock, alarm [ə lärm′ klŏk′] 26/13
clogged drain [klŏgd′ drān′] 33/11
close the window [klōz′ dhə wĭn′dō] 3/I
closet [klŏz′ət] 26/1
cloth [klŏth] 30/5
Clothes, Basic [bā′sĭk klōz′] 48
Clothes, Casual [kăzh′ ə wəl klōz′] 49
Clothes, Cold Weather
  [kōld′ wĕdh′ ər klōz′] 50
Clothes, Describing [dĭs krī′bĭng klōz′] 52–53
clothes, look at the [lŏŏk′ ăt dhə klōz′] 73/H
clothes, sell [sĕl′ klōz′] 88/G
Clothes, Taking Care of
  [tā′kĭng kër əv klōz′] 56–57
cloudy [klow′dē] 8/5
coat [kōt] 50/11
cockroaches [kŏk′ rōch əz] 33/13
coffee [kŏ′fē] 38/11
coffee, jar of [jär′ əv kŏ′fē] 37/7
coffee table [kŏ′fē tā′bəl] 24/9
coins [koynz] 10/3
cold [kōld] 8/12, 62/1
collect fares [kə lĕkt′ fërz′] 89/V
collect garbage [kə lĕkt′ gär′bĭj] 89/U
collect tickets [kə lĕkt′ tĭk′əts] 89/W
Colorado [kŏl′ ə rŏd′ ō] 98/6
Colors [kŭl′ərz] 9
comb [kōm] 61/1
comb . . . hair [kōm′. . . hër′] 14/F
come home [kŭm′ hōm′] 15/M
come in [kŭm′ in′] 3/D
come out of the store
  [kŭm owt′ əv dhə stör′] 73/A
Community [kə myŏŏ′nə tē] 68–69
computer [kəm pyŏŏ′tər] 2/13
computer, work at the
  [würk′ ăt dhə kəm pyŏŏ′tər] 3/G
computer programmer
  [kəm pyŏŏ′tər prŏ′grăm ər] 86/4
conductor [kən dŭk′tər] 85/23
Connecticut [kə nĕ′tĭ kət] 98/7
Construction Site [kən strŭk′shən sīt′] 87
construction worker
  [kən strŭk′shən wür′kər] 84/7
container of yogurt
  [kən tā′nər əv yō′gərt] 37/2
Continents [kŏn′tə nənts] 96
cook [kŏŏk] 43/1
cook dinner [kŏŏk′ dĭn′ər] 15/N
cookies [kŏŏk′ēz] 39/21

cookies, package of
  [păk′ ĭj əv kŏŏk′ēz] 37/4
Cooking a Meal [kŏŏk′ĭng ə mēl′] 46–47
cool [kŏŏl] 8/11
corn [körn] 34/5
corner [kör′nər] 72/5
costume, wear a [wër′ ə kŏs′tŏŏm] 95/M
cotton balls [kŏ′tən bölz′] 65/4
couch [kowch] 24/11
cough [köf] 63/B
counter [kown′tər] 25/14
courthouse [kört′hows′] 68/3
cousins [kŭz′ənz] 16/8
cracked ceiling [krăkt′ sē′lĭng] 32/4
cracked wall [krăkt′ wöl] 32/2
cradle [krā′dəl] 90/12
crawl [kröl] 91/D
cream [krēm] 38/2, 64/3
credit card [krĕd′ĭt kärd′] 10/9
crib [krĭb] 90/10
cross the street [krös′ dhə strēt′] 73/E
crosswalk [krös′wök′] 72/3
crutches [krŭch′əz] 65/8
cry [krī] 91/J
cucumber [kyŏŏ′kŭm bər] 34/10
cup [kŭp] 42/7, 101
cup, a half [ə hăf′ kŭp′] 101
cup, a quarter [ə kwör′tər kŭp′] 101
cup, a third of a [ə thürd′ əv ə kŭp′] 101
curb [kürb] 72/10
curly hair [kür′lē hër′] 13/16
curtain, shower [show′ər kür′tən] 27/2
curtains [kür′tənz] 26/5
custodian [kŭs tō′dē ən] 84/8
customer [kŭs tə′mər] 40/5
cut [kŭt] 62/8
cut broccoli [kŭt′ brŏk′lē] 46/C
cut grass [kŭt′ grăs′] 88/F
cut hair [kŭt′ hër′] 88/D
cut meat [kŭt′ mēt′] 88/E
cut the cake [kŭt′ dhə kāk′] 17/I

D
Daily Routines [dā′lē rŏŏ tēnz′] 14–15
Dairy Products [dër′ē prŏd′ŭkts] 38–39
dancer [dăn′sər] 86/13
dark blue [därk′ blŏŏ′] 9/17
dashboard [dăsh′börd′] 77/9
date [dāt] 70/7
daughter [dö′tər] 16/13
day [dā] 5/14

Day, Times of [tīmz′ əv dā′]   6
Day-Care Center [dā′kër′ sĕn′tər]   90–91
day-care worker [dā′kër′ wür′kər]   90/I
December [dē sĕm′bər]   4/12
deck [dĕk]   22/10
decorate the tree [dĕk′ə rāt dhə trē′]   95/T
Delaware [dĕl′ə wăr′]   98/8
deliver groceries [də lĭv′ər grō′sə rēz]   89/S
deliver mail [də lĭv′ər māl′]   89/R
deliver packages [də lĭv′ər păk′ĭj əz]   89/T
delivery person [də lĭv′ər ē pür′sən]   83/20
dental assistant [dĕn′təl ə sĭs′tənt]   83/15
dentist [dĕn′tĭst]   83/14
deodorant [dē ōd′ə rənt]   61/10
depart [də pärt′]   81/B
Department of Motor Vehicles
    [də pärt′mənt əv mō′tər vē′ə kəlz]   69/16
department store [də pärt′mənt stör′]   69/20
deposit slip [də pŏz′ət slĭp′]   70/11
Describing Clothes [də skrī′bĭng klōz′]   52–53
Describing People [də skrī′bĭng pē′pəl]   12–13
desk [dĕsk]   2/7
detergent [dĭ tür′jənt]   56/2
diaper [dī′pər]   90/6
diapers, change [chānj′ dī′pərz]   91/B
die [dī]   21/L
diet, go on a [gō′ ŏn ə dī′ət]   64/G
dig [dĭg]   87/C
dime [dīm]   10/6
dinner, cook [kŏŏk′ dĭn′ər]   15/N
Directions [dĭ rĕk′shənz]   97
dirty [dür′tē]   52/6
dishes, dry the [drī′ dhə dĭsh′əz]   28/G
dishes, wash the [wŏsh′ dhə dĭsh′əz]   28/F
dishwasher [dĭsh′wŏsh′ər]   43/2
Distance [dĭs′təns]   101
District of Columbia
    [dĭs′trĭkt əv kə lŭm′bē ə]   99/51
divorced, get
    [gĕt′ dĭ′vörst]   21/H
DMV
    [dē ĕm vē′]   69/16
do alterations [dōō′ öl′tə rā′shənz]   57/D
do the laundry [dōō′ dhə lön′drē]   29/P
doctor [dŏk′tər]   66/6
dollar [dŏl′ər]   10/2
donuts [dō′nŭts]   44/9
door, front [frŭnt′ dör′]   22/4
doorman [dör′mān′]   84/11
down [down]   79/5
down vest [down′ vĕst′]   50/2

drain [drān]   27/4
drain, clogged [klŏgd′ drān′]   33/11
drapes [drāps]   24/4
drawer [drör]   26/3
dress [drĕs]   48/I, 91/L
dresser [drĕs′ər]   26/2
dried beans [drīd′ bēnz′]   39/16
drill [drĭl]   31/6
drink champagne [drĭngk′ shăm pān′]   94/A
drink milk [drĭngk′ mĭlk′]   17/H
dripping faucet [drĭp′ĭng fö′sĭt]   33/10
drive a bus [drīv′ ə bŭs′]   89/O
drive a cab [drīv′ ə kăb′]   89/P
drive a truck [drīv′ ə trŭk′]   89/Q
driver, bus [bŭs′drī′vər]   85/15
driver, taxi [tăk′sī drī′vər]   84/12
driver, truck [trŭk′drī′vər]   85/19
drive-thru window [drīv′throo wĭn′dō]   70/2
driveway [drīv′wā′]   22/7
drop off [drŏp′ öf′]   91/A
dropper, medicine [mĕd′ə sən drŏp′ər]   64/6
drops [drŏps]   64/5
drown [drown]   75/C
druggist [drŭg′ĭst]   82/I
drugs [drŭgz]   64/I
drugstore [drŭg′stör′]   82/2
dry [drī]   53/12
Dry Cleaner [drī′klē′nər]   57
dry the dishes [drī′ dhə dĭsh′əz]   28/G
dry [drī′ər]   56/3
dust the furniture [dŭst′ dhə für′nə chər]   28/E
dustpan [dŭst′ păn′]   30/3

E
ear [ïr]   60/3
earache [ïr′āk′]   62/7
earmuffs [ïr′mŭfs′]   50/14
earrings [ïr′ĭngz]   55/3
earthquake [ürth′kwāk′]   74/11
east [ēst]   97/17
Easter [ē′stər]   94
Easter egg hunt, go on an
    [gō′ ŏn ən ē′stər ĕg hŭnt′]   94/F
Easter eggs, paint
    [pānt′ ē′stər ĕgz′]   94/E
easy chair [ē′zē chër′]   24/5
eat a big meal [ēt′ ə bĭg′ mēl′]   95/Q
eat breakfast [ēt′ brĕk′fəst]   15/I
eggs [ĕgz]   38/4
eggs, fried [frīd′ ĕgz′]   44/3
eggs, scrambled [skrăm′bəld ĕgz′]   44/I

elbow [ĕl′bō] 59/17
electrician [ĭ lĕk trĭ′shən] 84/2
elevator [ĕl′ə vā′tər] 23/10
embarrassed [ĭm băr′əst] 19/13
Emergencies [ĭ mür′jən sēz] 74–75
empty the wastebasket
   [ĕm′tē dhə wāst′bās′kət] 29/K
end table [ĕnd′ tā′bəl] 24/8
English muffin [ĭng′lĭsh mŭf′ən] 44/5
entrance [ĕn′trəns] 23/5
envelope [ĕn′və lōp′] 71/6
eraser [ĭ rā′sər] 2/3
Europe [yŏŏr′əp] 96/3
evening [ēv′nĭng] 6/3
examine the patient
   [ĭg zăm′ĭn dhə pā′shənt] 67/F
examining room [ĭg zăm′ə nĭng rōōm′] 66/8
excited [ĭk sĭt′əd] 18/7
exercise [ĕk′sər sīz] 64/F, 93
exit [ĕg′zĭt] 23/4
extra-large [ĕk′strə lärj′] 53/20
eye [ī] 60/5
eyebrow [ī′brow′] 60/4

F
face [fās] 58/1, 60
factory worker [făk′tə rē würk′ər] 85/13
faint [fānt] 63/C
fall [föl] 4/16, 75/A
fall down [föl′ down′] 75/A
fall in love [föl′ ĭn lŭv′] 21/F
Family [făm′ə lē] 16
family and friends, get together with
   [gĕt′ tə gĕdh′ər wĭth
   făm′lē ănd frĕndz′] 95/O
fares, collect [kə lĕkt′ fĕrz′] 89/V
farmer [färm′ər] 85/20
fat [făt] 12/4
father [fŏdh′ər] 16/2
faucet [fö′sĭt] 27/3
faucet, dripping [drĭp′ĭng fö′sĭt] 33/10
February [fĕb′rōō ĕr′ē] 4/2
feed [fēd] 91/F
feelings [fē′lĭngz] 18–19
fever [fē′vər] 62/2
file clerk [fīl′ klürk′] 86/3
fill out the form [fĭl′ owt′ dhə förm′] 67/A
finger [fĭng′gər] 58/8
fire [fīr] 74/2
fire escape [fīr′ə skāp′] 23/3
fire exit [fīr′ ĕg′zĭt] 23/4

fire fighter [fīr′ fī′tər] 74/3
firehouse [fīr′hows′] 68/2
fireworks, watch [wŏch′ fīr′würks′] 95/K
First Aid [fürst′ ād′] 65
fish [fĭsh] 36/10
fish, broil [broyl′ fĭsh′] 47/M
fisherman [fĭsh′ər mən] 85/18
fix appliances [fĭks′ ə plī′əns əz] 88/A
fix cars [fĭks′ kärz′] 88/B
fix pipes [fĭks′ pīps′] 88/C
fix TVs [fĭks′ tē vēz′] 88/A
flag, wave a [wāv′ ə flăg′] 94/G
flashlight [flăsh′ līt′] 31/8
flight attendant [flīt′ ə tĕn′dənt] 80/7
flood [flŭd] 74/10
flooded basement [flŭd′əd bās′mənt] 33/15
floor [flör] 23/2, 24/3
floor, mop the [mŏp′ dhə flör′] 29/O
floor, sweep the [swēp′ dhə flör′] 29/M
Florida [flör′ə də] 98/9
florist [flör′ĭst] 68/9
flour [flow′ər] 38/13
flour, bag of [băg′ əv flow′ər] 37/6
flowers, get [gĕt′ flow′ərz] 94/D
foggy [fŏg′ē] 8/7
fold [fōld] 56/D
food [fōōd] 34–39
Foods, Prepared [prē pĕrd′ fōōdz′] 44–45
foot [fŏŏt] 59/21
football, play [plā′ fŏŏt′böl′] 92/D
foot/feet [fŏŏt] [fēt] 101
forehead [för′hĕd′] 60/2
foreman [för′mən] 85/14
fork [förk] 42/11
form, fill out the [fĭl′ owt′ dhə förm′] 67/A
Fourth of July [förth′ əv jŏŏ lī′] 95
freezer [frē′zər] 25/15
freezing [frē′zĭng] 8/13
french fries [frĕnch′ frīz′] 44/12
Friday [frī′dā] 5/6
fried chicken [frīd′ chĭk′ən] 45/20
fried eggs [frīd′ ĕgz′] 44/3
friends, get together with family and
   [gĕt′ tə gĕdh′ər wĭth făm′ lē
   ănd frĕndz′] 95/O
from [frŭm] 78/3
front door [frŭnt′ dör′] 22/4
fruit and vegetable market
   [frōōt′ ănd vej′tə bəl mär′kət] 83/18
fruits [frōōts] 35

fry onions and peppers
[frī′ ŭn′yənz ănd pĕp′ərz]   46/F
frying pan [frī′ĭng păn′]   25/5
furniture, build [bĭld′ für′nə chər]   88/K
furniture, dust the [dŭst′ dhə für′nə chər]   28/E

G
gallon [găl′ən]   101
garage [gə rŏj′]   22/6
garage, parking [pär′kĭng gə rŏj′]   69/15
garbage, collect [kə lĕkt′ gär′bĭj]   89/U
garbage, take out the
[tāk′ owt′ dhə gär′bĭj]   28/J
garbage can [gär′bĭj kăn′]   22/9
garden [gär′dən]   22/13
gardener [gärd′nər]   84/5
garlic [gär′lĭk]   34/6
gas pedal [găs′ pĕd′ əl]   77/13
gas station [găs′ stā′shən]   82/5
gas tank [găs′ tănk′]   77/7
gate [gāt]   80/6
Georgia [jör′jə]   98/10
get a cast [gĕt′ ə kăst′]   64/E
get a job [gĕt′ ə jŏb′]   20/D
get divorced [gĕt′ dĭ vörst′]   21/H
get dressed [gĕt′ drĕst′]   14/H
get flowers [gĕt′ flow′ərz]   94/D
get married [gĕt′ măr′ēd]   21/G
get rest [gĕt′ rĕst′]   64/B
get sick [gĕt′ sĭk′]   21/K
get stitches [gĕt′ stĭch′əz]   64/C
get together with family and friends
[gĕt′ tə gĕdh′ər wĭth
făm′lē ănd frĕndz′]   95/O
get up [gĕt′ up′]   14/B
girl [gürl]   11/2
give a present to [gĭv′ ə prĕz′ənt tōō]   17/A
give a shot [gĭv′ ə shŏt′]   67/I
give an injection [gĭv′ ən ĭn jĕk′shən]   67/I
give thanks [gĭv′ thănks′]   95/P
give valentines [gĭv′ văl′ən tīnz]   94/C
glass [glăs]   42/6
glasses [glăs′əz]   55/8
gloves [glŭvz]   50/13
gloves, rubber [rŭb′ər glŭvz′]   30/7
go camping [gō′ kăm′pĭng]   92/A
go Christmas shopping
[gō′ krĭs′məs shŏp′ĭng]   95/S
go hiking [gō′ hī′kĭng]   92/B
go into the store [gō′ ĭn tə dhə stör′]   73/B
go on a diet [gō′ ŏn ə dī′ət]   64/G

go on an Easter egg hunt
[gō′ ŏn ən ē′stər ĕg hŭnt′]   94/F
go out [gō′ owt′]   3/C
go running [gō′ rŭn′ĭng]   93/N
go skiing [gō′ skē′ ĭng]   92/H
go swimming [gō′ swĭ′mĭng]   93/M
go to bed [gō′ tə bĕd′]   15/O
go to sleep [gō′ tə slēp′]   15/P
go to the movies [gō′ tə dhə mōō′vēz]   93/J
go trick-or-treating [gō′ trĭk ər trē′tĭng]   95/N
good-bye, wave [wāv′ gŏŏd bī′]   81/C
graduate [grăj′ə wāt′]   20/C
gram [grăm]   101
grand parents [grănd′ păr′ ənts]   16/1
grapefruit [grāp′frōōt′]   35/6
grapes [grāps]   35/2
grass, cut [kŭt′ grăs′]   88/F
grate cheese [grāt′ chēz′]   46/H
gray [grā]   9/11
gray hair [grā′ hër′]   13/21
green [grēn]   9/9
grocer [grō′sər]   83/17
groceries [grō′sə rēz]   40/10
groceries, buy [bī′ grō′sə rēz]   73/G
groceries, deliver [də lĭv′ ər grō′sə rēz]   89/S
ground meat [grownd′ mēt′]   36/3
grounds, take care of
[tāk′ kër′ əv growndz′]   89/N

H
Hair   13
hair [hër]   60/1
hair, cut [kŭt′ hër′]   88/D
hairdresser [hër′drĕs′ ər]   82/8
hairstylist [hër′stī′lĭst]   82/8
half cup, a [ə hăf′ kŭp′]   101
hall [höl]   23/8
Halloween [hŏl′ə wēn′]   95
ham [hăm]   36/6
hamburger [hăm′bür′gər]   44/11
hammer [hăm′ər]   31/4, 87/H
hamper [hăm′pər]   27/10
hand [hănd]   58/5
hands, shake [shāk′ hăndz′]   81/F
hang up [hăng′ ŭp′]   57/B
hanger [hăng′ər]   57/9
happy [hăp′ē]   18/2
hat [hăt]   50/4
have a baby [hăv′ ə bā′bē]   21/I
have a barbecue [hăv′ ə bär′bə kyōō′]   95/J

have a heart attack

   [hăv′ ə härt′ ə tăk′]   75/B

have a picnic [hăv′ ə pĭk′nĭk]   95/J

have an operation

   [hăv′ ən ŏp′ ə rā′shən]   64/A

Hawaii [hə wŏ′ē]   98/11

Head [hĕd]   60

head [hĕd]   58/11

headache [hĕd′āk′]   62/3

headlights [hĕd′līts′]   77/2

Health Care Items [hĕlth′ kër′ ī′təmz]   65

heart [härt]   59/26

heart attack, have a

   [hăv′ ə härt′ ə tăk′]   75/B

heat, no [nō′hēt′]   32/5

heating pad [hē′tĭng păd′]   65/6

heavy [hĕv′ē]   12/4, 52/1

heel [hēl]   59/22

Height [hīt]   12/101

high [hī]   52/7

high blood pressure [hī′ blŭd′ prĕsh′ ər]   63/13

high chair [hī′ chër′]   43/9

hiking, go [gō′ hī′kĭng]   92/B

hip [hĭp]   58/7

hold [hōld]   91/I

Holidays, Celebrate the

   [sĕl′ ə brāt′dhə hŏl′ə dāz]   94–95

home, come [kŭm′ hōm′]   15/M

homesick [hōm′ sĭk′]   19/14

hood [hŏŏd]   77/4

hose [hōz]   31/11

hot [hŏt]   8/9

hot dog [hŏt′ dög′]   44/13

hot water, no [nō′ hŏt′ wŏ′tər]   32/7

hot water, bottle [hŏt′ wŏt′ ər bŏt′əl]   65/7

house, leave the [lēv′ dhə hows′]   15/J

Household Problems

   [hows′hōld′ prŏb′ləmz]   32–33

housekeeper [hows′kē′ pər]   84/4

houses, build [bĭld′ how′zəz]   88/J

Houses and Surroundings

   [how′zəz ənd sə rown′dĭngz]   22

Housework [hows′würk′]   28–29

hug [hŭg]   81/G

hungry [hŭng′grē]   19/11

hurricane [hür′ə kăn]   74/13

husband [hŭs′bənd]   16/9

I

ice cream [īs′ krēm′]   45/21

ice pack [īs′ păk′]   65/5

icy [īs′sē]   8/6

ID card [ī′ dē′ kärd′]   55/10

Idaho [ī′də hō′]   98/12

ignition [ĭg nĭsh′ən]   77/11

Illinois [ĭl′ ə noy′]   98/13

in [ĭn]   54/6

in front of [ĭn frŭnt′əv]   54/7

inch [ĭnch]   101

Indian Ocean [ĭn′dē ən ō′shən]   96/13

Indiana [ĭn′dē ăn′ə]   98/14

Indoor Activities [ĭn′dör ăk tĭv′ ə tēz]   93

infected toe [ĭn fĕk′təd tō′]   63/16

ingredients, mix [mĭks′ ĭn grē′dē ənts]   47/K

injection [ĭn jĕk′shən]   64/4

injection, give an [gĭv′ ən ĭn jĕk′shən]   67/I

Injuries [ĭn′jə rēz]   62–63

insect bite [ĭn′sĕkt bīt′]   62/11

instrument, play an

   [plā′ ən ĭn′strə mənt]   93/I

insurance card [ĭn shŏŏr′əns kärd′]   66/4

insurance card, show

   [shō′ ĭn shŏŏr′əns kärd′]   67/D

insurance form [ĭn shŏŏr′əns förm′]   66/3

intercom [ĭn′tər kŏm′]   23/13

Intersection [ĭn′tər sĕk′shən]   72–73

intersection [ĭn′tər sĕk′shən]   72/6

into [ĭn′tŏŏ]   79/8

Iowa [ī′ə wə]   98/15

iron [ī′ərn]   56/7, 56/C

ironing board [ī′ər nĭng börd′]   56/6

J

jacket [jăk′ət]   50/1

janitor [jăn′ ə tər]   84/8

January [jăn′yŏŏ ër′ ē]   4/1

jar of coffee [jär′əv kö′fē]   37/7

jeans [jēnz]   49/4

Jewelry [jŏŏ′lə rē]   55

job, get a [gĕt′ ə jŏb′]   20/D

juice [jŏŏs]   39/20

July [jŏŏ lī]   4/7

June [jŏŏn]   4/6

K

Kansas [kăn′zəs]   98/16

Kentucky [kĕn tŭk′ē]   98/17

ketchup [kĕch′əp]   39/25

kettle [kĕt′əl]   25/3

kilogram [kĭl′ə grăm′]   101

kilometer [kĭ lŏm′ə tər]   101

kiss [kĭs]   17/C

Kitchen [kǐch′ən]   25
kitchen sink [kǐch′ən sǐngk′]   25/10
knee [nē]   59/18
knife [nīf]   42/12

L
ladder [lăd′ər]   31/10
lamb [lăm]   36/7
lamp [lămp]   24/6
large [lärj]   12/7, 53/19
laugh [lăf]   17/B
Laundromat [lön′drə măt]   56
laundry, do the [dōō′ dhə lön′drē]   29/P
laundry basket [lön′drē băs′kət]   56/5
lawn [lön]   22/8
lawn, mow the [mō′ dhə lön′]   29/R
lawn mower [lön′ mō′ər]   31/14
lawyer [lö′yər]   86/10
lay [lā]   87/E
leaking ceiling [lē′kǐng sē′lǐng]   32/1
leaking roof [lē′kǐng rōōf′]   32/1
learn [lürn]   15/L
leave [lēv]   81/B
leave the house [lēv′ dhə hows′]   15/J
leaves, rake the [rāk′ dhə lēvz′]   28/I
leg [lěg]   58/14
Leisure [lē′zhər]   92–93
lemons [lě′mənz]   35/7
Length [lěngkth]   101
lengthen [lěng′thən]   57/E
letter [lět′ər]   71/5
letter, mail a [māl′ ə lět′ər]   73/F
letter carrier [lět′ər kăr′ē yər]   71/3
lettuce [lět′əs]   34/3
librarian [lî′brër′ē ən]   83/12
library [lī′brër′ē]   83/13
license plate [lī′səns plāt′]   77/1
Life Events [līf′ ə věnts′]   20–21
light [līt]   52/2
light blue [līt′ blōō′]   9/16
limes [līmz]   35/8
line [līn]   70/5
lip [lǐp]   60/10
Liquid Measure [lǐk′wǐd mězh′ər]   101
listen [lǐs′ən]   3/F
listen to music [lǐs′ən tə myōō′zǐk]   93/L
liter [lět′ər]   101
little [lǐt′əl]   12/8
Living Room [lǐv′ǐng rōōm′]   24
load [lōd]   56/A
loaf of bread [lōf′ əv brěd′]   37/5

lobby [lŏb′ē]   23/9
lobster [lŏb′stər]   36/11
lock, broken [brō′kən lŏk′]   32/8
locksmith [lŏk′ smǐth′]   84/3
long [löng]   53/13
long hair [löng′ hër′]   13/11
look at the clothes [lōōk′ ăt dhə klōz′]   73/H
look at the screen [lōōk′ ăt dhə skrēn′]   3/H
look at the windows
     [lōōk′ ăt dhə wǐn′dōz]   73/H
loose [lōōs]   53/16
Louisiana [lōō wē′zē ăn′ə]   98/18
love, fall in [föl′ ǐn lŭv′]   21/F
low [lō]   52/8
luggage [lŭg′əj]   80/3
lung [lŭng]   59/25

M
mail, deliver [də lǐv′ər māl′]   89/R
mail a letter [māl′ ə lět′ər]   73/F
mailbox [māl′ bŏks′]   71/4
mailboxes [māl′bŏks′əz]   23/11
Maine [mān]   98/19
maintenance man [mān′tə nənts măn′]   85/17
make a phone call [māk′ ə fōn′ köl′]   73/C
make a toast [māk′ ə tōst′]   94/B
make the bed [māk′ dhə běd′]   28/A
mall [möl]   69/19
man [măn]   11/5
Maps [măps]   96–99
March [märch]   4/3
margarine [mär′jə rǐn]   38/7
market, fruit and vegetable
     [frōōt′ ănd vej′tə bəl mär′kət]   83/18
married, get [get′ măr′ēd]   21/G
Maryland [mër′ə lənd]   98/20
mashed potatoes [măsht′ pə tā′tōz]   45/19
Massachusetts [măs′ə chōō′sǐts]   98/21
May [mā]   4/5
mayonnaise [mā′ ə nāz′]   39/26
Meal, Cooking a [kōōk′ǐng ə mēl′]   46–47
measure [mězhz′ər]   87/G
Measures [mězhz′ərz]   101
measuring tape [mězhz′ə rǐng tāp′]   101
Meat [mēt]   36
meat, cut [kŭt′ mēt′]   88/E
meat, ground [grownd′ mēt′]   36/3
mechanic [mə kăn′ ǐk]   82/3
Medical Office [měd′ə kəl ö′fǐs]   66–67
medicine [měd′ə sən]   64/1
medicine, take [tāk′ měd′ə sən]   64/D

sleep, go to [gō′ tə slēp′]   15/P
Sleepwear [slēp′wër′]   51
slice onions [slīs′ŭn′yənz]   46/D
slippers [slĭp′ərz]   51/12
slot [slŏt]   56/4
small [smöl]   12/8, 53/17
smile [smīl]   17/D
smoke [smōk]   74/1
smoking sections [smō′kĭng sek′shən] 43/10
sneakers [snē′kərz]   49/8
sneeze [snēz]   63/A
snowing [snō′ĭng]   8/2
soap, bar of [bär′ əv sōp′]   37/11
soccer, play [plā′ sŏk′ər]   92/F
socks [sŏks]   51/8
soda [sō′də]   39/19
soda, bottle of [bŏt′əl əv sō′də]   37/3
sofa [sō′fə]   24/11
soldier [sōl′jər]   85/21
Solid Weights [sŏl′əd wāts′]   101
son [sŭn]   16/12
sore throat [sör′ thrōt′]   63/12
soup [sōōp]   39/18
soup, can of [kăn′ əv sōōp′]   37/8
south [sowth]   97/16
South America [sowth′ ə mёr′ə kə]   96/5
South Atlantic Ocean
    [sowth′ ăt lăn′tĭk ō′shən]   96/12
South Carolina [sowth′ kăr′ ə lī′nə] 99/40
South Dakota [sowth′ də kō′tə]   99/41
South Pacific Ocean
    [sowth′ pə sĭf′ ĭk ō′shən]   96/10
southeast [sowth ēst′]   97/21
southwest [sowth wĕst′]   97/22
spaghetti [spə gĕt′ē]   39/17, 45/15
spinach [spĭn′əch]   34/4
sponge [spŭnj]   30/9
Spoon [spōōn]   42/13
sports [spörts]   92
spray [sprā]   64/7
spring [sprĭng]   4/14
square [skwёr]   9/3
stairs [stёrz]   23/12
stairway [stёr′wā′]   23/12
stamp [stămp]   71/8
stand [stănd]   3/N
stars [stärz]   6/7
start school [stärt′skōōl′]   20/B
steak [stāk′]   36/2
steam vegetables [stēm′ vĕj′tə bəlz] 47/I
steering wheel [stïr′ĭng wēl′]   77/10

stepladder [stĕp′ lăd′ ər]   31/10
steps [stĕps]   23/6
steps, broken [brō′kən stĕps′]   33/9
stereo [stёr′ē ō]   24/13
stereo system [stёr′ē ō sĭs′təm]   24/13
stir onions and peppers
    [stür′ŭn′yənz ənd pĕp′ərz]   46/G
stitches, get [gĕt′stĭch′əz]   64/C
stockings [stŏk′ ĭngz]   51/6
stomach [stŭm′ək]   59/27
stomachache [stŭm′ək āk′]   62/5
stop [stŏp]   73/D
stopped-up toilet [stŏpt′ ŭp′ ïoy′lət] 32/6
stove [stōv]   25/6
straight hair [strāt′ hёr′]   13/14
straighten up the room
    [strā′tən ŭp′ dhə rōōm′]   28/B
strawberries [strö′bёr′ ēz]   35/11
street, cross the [krös′ dhə strēt′] 73/E
string beans [strĭng′ bēnz′]   34/7
stroller [strō′lər]   90/2
student [stōō′dənt]   2/5
study [stŭd′ē]   15/L
subway [sŭb′wā′]   76/7
sugar [shŏŏg′ ər]   38/3
suit [sōōt]   48/9
suitcase [sōōt′kās′]   80/3
summer [sŭm′ər]   4/15
sun [sŭn]   6/5
Sunday [sŭn′dā]   5/1
sunglasses [sŭn′glăs′ əz]   49/3
sunny [sŭn′ē]   8/4
superintendent [sōō′ pər ĭn tĕn′dənt] 84/10
Supermarket [sōō′pər mär′ kət]   40–41
supermarket [sōō′pər mär′ kət]   68/11
surprised [sər prīzd′]   19/8
swallow poison [swŏl′ō poy′zən]   75/D
sweater [swĕt′ ər]   50/3
sweatshirt [swĕt′shürt′]   50/5
sweep the floor [swēp′ dhə flör′]   29/M
swimming, go [gō′ swĭm′ĭng]   93/M
swimsuit [swĭm′sōōt′]   49/1
swimtrunks [swĭm′trŭnks′]   49/2
swollen ankle [swō′lən ăng′kəl]   63/15
syrup [sïr′əp]   44/8

T
table [tā′bəl]   42/1
table, coffee [kö′fē tā′bəl]   24/9
table, end [ĕnd′ tā′bəl]   24/8
table, night [nīt′ tā′ bəl]   26/14

Table Setting [tā′bəl sĕt′ĭng]   42
tablespoon [tā′bəl spoon′]   101
Tailor [tā′lər]   57
tailor [tā′lər]   57/8
take a nap [tāk′ ə năp′]   91/G
take a picture [tāk′ ə pĭk′chər]   17/G
take a shower [tāk′ ə show′ər]   14/C
take care of children
   [tāk′ kër′ əv chĭld′rən]   89/L
take care of grounds
   [tāk′ kër′ əv growndz′]   89/N
take care of pools
   [tāk′ kër′ əv poolz′]   89/M
take medicine [tāk′ mĕd′ə sən]   64/D
take out [tāk′ owt′]   41/F, 56/B, 87/A
take out the garbage
   [tāk′ owt′ dhə gär′bĭj]   28/J
take . . . temperature
   [tāk′ . . . tĕm′pər ə chər]   67/H
talk [tök]   3/L
tall [töl]   12/I
tape measure [tāp′ mĕzh′ ər]   31/7
taxi [tăk′sē]   76/6
taxi driver [tăk′sē drī′vər]   84/12
taxicab [tăk′sē kăb′]   76/6
tea [tē]   38/12
teacher [tē′chər]   2/4
teakettle [tē′kĕt′əl]   25/3
teaspoon [tē′spoon′]   101
teenager [tēn′ā′jər]   11/7
telephone [tĕl′ə fōn′]   24/7
telephone, public [pŭb′lĭk tĕ′lə fōn′]   72/4
television [tĕl′ə vĭzh′ən]   24/14
teller [tĕl′ər]   70/I
temperature [tĕm′pər ə chər]   8/8
Tennessee [tĕn′ə sē′]   99/42
tennis, play [plā′ tĕn′əs]   92/C
Texas [tĕk′səs]   99/43
Thanksgiving [thăngks gĭv′ ĭng]   95
theft [thĕft]   74/7
thermometer [thər möm′ə tər]   65/3
thigh [thī]   59/16
thin [thĭn]   12/6
third of a cup, a [ə thürd ′əv ə kŭp′]   101
thirsty [thürs′tē]   19/12
thread [thrĕd]   57/2
through [throo]   78/4
thumb [thŭm]   58/9
Thursday [thürz′dā]   5/5
ticket [tĭk′ət]   80/2
tickets, collect [kə lĕkt′ tĭk′əts]   89/W
tie [tī]   48/5
tight [tīt]   53/15
Time [tīm]   4–7
Times of Day [tīmz′ əv dā′]   6
tire [tīr]   77/8
tired [tīrd]   19/10
to [too]   78/2
toast [tōst]   44/4
toast, make a [māk′ ə tōst′]   94/B
toaster [tōs′tər]   25/13
today [tə dā′]   5/12
toe [tō]   59/23
toe, infected [ĭn fĕk′təd tō′]   63/16
toilet [toy′lət]   27/12
toilet, stopped-up [stŏpt′ ŭp′ toy′lət]   32/6
toilet paper [toy′lət pā′pər]   27/13
toilet paper, roll of
   [rōl′ əv toy′lət pā′pər]   37/9
Toiletries [toy′lə trēz]   61
tomato [tə mā′tō]   34/8
tomorrow [tə mör′ō]   5/13
tongue [tŭng]   60/12
toolbox [tool′ bŏks′]   31/9
Tools [toolz]   31
tooth [tooth]   60/11
toothache [tooth′ āk′]   62/6
toothbrush [tooth′ brŭsh′]   61/4
toothpaste [tooth′ pāst′]   61/3
toothpaste, tube of
   [toob′ əv tooth′ pāst′]   37/12
tornado [tör nā′dō]   74/12
toward [törd]   78/2
towel [tow′əl]   27/11
toy [toy]   90/7
traffic light [trăf′ək līt′]   72/I
train [trān]   76/9
train conductor [trān′ kən dŭk′tər]   85/23
train station [trān′ stā′shən]   69/14
Transportation [trăns′pər tā′shən]   76
trash can [trăsh′ kăn′]   25/11
Treatments [trēt′mənts]   64
tree, decorate the [dĕk′ə rāt dhə trē′]   95/T
tree, plant a [plănt′ ə trē′]   29/Q
triangle [trī′ăng′gəl]   9/2
trick-or-treating, go [gō′ trĭk′ər trē′tĭng]   95/N
truck [trŭk]   76/3
truck, drive a [drīv′ ə trŭk′]   89/Q
truck driver [trŭk′ drīv′ ər]   85/19
trunk [trŭngk]   77/6
try on [trī′ ŏn′]   57/C
T-shirt [tē′shürt′]   49/7

tube of toothpaste
    [tōob′ əv tōoth′ pāst′]   37/12
Tuesday [tōoz′dā]   5/3
turkey [tür′kē]   36/9
turn [türn]   73/J
TV [tē vē′]   24/14
TV, watch [wŏch′ tē vē′]   93/K
TVs, fix [fĭks′ tē vēz′]   88/A
TVs, repair [rə për′ tē vēz′]   88/A
typist [tī′pəst]   86/2

U
umbrella [ŭm brĕl′ə]   50/9
uncle [ŭng′kəl]   16/6
under [ŭn′dər]   54/9
underpants [ŭn′dər pănts′]   51/3
undershirt [ŭn′dər shürt′]   51/1
Underwear [ŭn′dər wër′]   51
uniform [yōo′nə förm′]   48/11
United States of America, the
    [dhə yōo nī′təd stāts′
    əv ə mër′ə kə]   98–99
unload [ŭn lōd′]   56/B
up [ŭp]   79/6
Utah [yōo′tö]   99/44

V
vacuum cleaner [văk′yōom klē′nər]   30/4
vacuum the rug [văk′yōom dhə rŭg′]   28/D
valentines, give [gĭv′ văl′ən tīnz′]   94/C
Valentine's Day [văl′ən tīnz′ dā′]   94
van [văn]   76/4
vegetable market, fruit and
    [frōot′ ănd vej′tə bəl mär′kət]   83/18
Vegetables [vej′tə bəlz]   34
vegetables, sell [sĕl′ vej′tə bəlz]   88/H
vegetables, steam [stēm′ vej′tə bəlz]   47/I
Vermont [vür mŏnt′]   99/45
vest [vĕst]   50/2
Virginia [vər jĭn′yə]   99/46
visit a cemetery [vĭz′ət ə sĕm′ə tër′ē]   94/I

W
waffles [wŏf′əlz]   44/6
waist [wāst]   58/6
wait [wāt]   67/E
wait for the bus [wāt′ för dhə bŭs′]   73/K
waiter [wā′tər]   43/6
waiting room [wā′tĭng rōom′]   66/1
waitress [wā′trəs]   43/7
wake up [wāk′ ŭp′]   14/A

walk [wök]   73/I
walker [wök′ər]   65/9
wall [wöl]   24/2
wall, cracked [krăkt′ wöl′]   32/2
wallet [wŏl′ət]   55/9
warm [wörm]   8/10
warm-up suit [wörm′ŭp sōot′]   49/10
wash the dishes [wŏsh dhə dĭsh′əz]   28/F
wash the windows [wŏsh dhə wĭn′dōz]   29/N
washcloth [wŏsh′klöth′]   61/6
washer [wŏsh′ər]   56/1
wash . . . face [wŏsh′ . . . fās′]   14/E
washing machine [wŏsh′ ĭng mə shēn′]   56/1
Washington [wŏsh′ ĭng tən]   99/47
wastebasket [wāst′băs′kət]   27/6
wastebasket, empty the
    [em′tē dhə wāst′ băs′kət]   29/K
watch [wŏch]   55/6
watch a parade [wŏch′ ə pə rād′]   94/H
watch fireworks [wŏch′ fīr′würks′]   95/K
watch TV [wŏch′ tē vē′]   93/K
water [wŏ′tər]   43/4
water, boil [boyl′ wŏ′tər]   46/B
water the plants [wŏ′tər dhə plănts′]   28/H
watermelons [wŏ′tər mĕl′ənz]   35/13
wave [wāv]   81/C
wave a flag [wāv′ ə flăg′]   94/G
wave good-bye [wāv′ gŏod bī′]   81/C
wavy hair [wāv′ ē hër′]   13/15
wear a costume [wër′ ə kŏs′tyōom]   95/M
Weather [wĕdh′ər]   8
Wednesday [wĕnz′dā]   5/4
week [wēk]   5/15
weigh [wā]   41/G
weigh the patient [wā′ dhə pā′shənt]   67/G
Weight [wāt]   12
Weights [wāts]   101
west [wĕst]   97/18
West Virginia [wĕst′ vər jĭn′yə]   99/48
wet [wĕt]   53/11
wheelchair [wēl′chër′]   65/10
white [wīt]   9/5
wide [wīd]   52/10
wife [wīf]   16/10
window [wĭn′dō]   22/5
window, broken [brō′kən wĭn′dō]   32/3
window, close the [klōz′ dhə wĭn′dō]   3/I
window, drive-thru [drīv′thrōo wĭn′dō]   70/2
windows, look at the
    [lŏok′ ăt dhə wĭn′dōz]   73/H
windows, wash the [wŏsh dhə wĭn′dōz]   29/N

windshield [wĭnd′shēld′]   77/5
windy [wĭn′dē]   8/3
winter [wĭn′tər]   4/13
Wisconsin [wĭs kŏn′sən]   99/49
withdrawal slip [wĭdh dröl′ slĭp′]   70/10
woman [wŏŏm′ən]   11/4
word processor [würd′ prŏ′sĕs ər]   86/2
work [würk]   15/K, 88–89
work at the computer
   [würk′ ăt dhə kəm pyōō′tər]   3/G
Workplaces [würk′plā′səz]   82–83
World, the [dhə würld′]   96–97
worried [wür′ēd]   19/9
wrench [rĕnch]   31/2
wrist [rĭst]   58/10
write [rīt]   3/A
write a prescription
   [rīt′ ə prə skrĭp′shən]   67/J
Wyoming [wī ō′mĭng]   99/50

X
X ray [eks′rā′]   66/9

Y
yard [yärd]   101
yardstick [yärd′stĭk′]   101
year [yïr]   5/16
yellow [yĕl′ō]   9/8
yesterday [yĕs′tər dā]   5/11
yogurt [yō′gərt]   38/8
yogurt, container of
   [kən tā′nər əv yō′gərt]   37/2
young [yŭng]   13/22

Z
zip code [zĭp′kōd′]   71/10
zipper [zĭp′ər]   57/5

A

a través del banco	78/4
a la ciudad	78/2
abacero	83/17
abarrotero	83/17
abarrotes	40/10
abogado	86/10
abrazarse	81/G
abrelatas	25/9
abreviaciones	101
abrigo	50/11
abril	4/4
abrir un cuaderno	3/J
abrir una tarjeta	17/J
abuelos	16/1
aburrido	18/5
acampar	92/A
accesorios	55
accidente	74/4
aceite	38/14
acelerador	77/13
acera	72/9
acondicionador del aire	26/4
acortar	57/F
acostarse	15/O
actividades al aire libre	92
actividades bajo techo	93
actor	86/15
actriz	86/15
adolescente	11/7
adulto	11/8
afeitarse	14/G
Africa	96/2
agosto	4/8
agua	43/4
aguja	57/1
ahogarse	75/C
airoso	8/3
ajo	34/6
Alabama	98/1
alargar	57/E
Alaska	98/2
alfombra	24/10, 26/6
alimentar	91/F
alimentos	34–39, 44–47
alimentos preparados comunes	44–45
almejas	36/13
almíbar	44/8
almohada	26/8
alrededor del accidente	79/10
alta	12/1

alta presión	63/13
alto	52/7
amarillo	9/8
ambulancia	74/5
anaquel	40/1
anaranjado	9/12
anciana	13/24
ancha	52/10
andador	65/9
angosta	52/9
anillo	55/1
anochecer	6/3
Antártica	96/7
Antártico	96/14
anteojos	55/8
anteojos de sol	49/3
año	5/16
aparatos domésticos	88/A
aparcamiento	69/21
aprender	15/L
apretada	53/15
archivista	86/3
área de construcción	87
aretes	55/3
Arizona	98/3
Arkansas	98/4
arreglar aparatos domésticos	88/A
arreglar automóviles	88/B
arreglar plomería	88/C
arreglar teles	88/A
arroz	39/15
Artico	96/8
artículos de tocador	61
artículos para el cuidado de la salud	65
artista	86/16
asador	25/8
asalto	74/9
asar pescado	47/M
ascensor	23/10
Asia	96/1
asiento para niño	77/15
asistente	82/4
asistente dental	83/15
asoleadero	22/10
aspiradora	30/4
aspirar la alfombra	28/D
asustados	18/6
Atlántico Norte	96/11
Atlántico Sur	96/12
atomizador	64/7
Australia	96/6

Indice

autobús	76/2
automóvil	76/1
auxiliar de vuelo	80/7
avergonzado	19/13
avión	76/8
ayer	5/11
ayuntamiento	69/12
azúcar	38/3
azul	9/7

B

babero	90/8
bailarín	86/13
bailarina	86/13
baja	12/3
bajando la colina	79/5
bajo	52/8
balanza	40/7
balcón	23/1
banca	72/12
bañera	27/5
baño	27
barba	13/9
barbería	82/11
barbero	82/10
barco	76/10
barra de jabón	37/11
barrer el piso	29/M
báscula	40/7
basurero	22/9, 25/11, 27/6
bata de baño	51/11
bata de noche	51/9
batería	77/3
baúl	77/6
bebé	11/1
beber champaña	94/A
beber leche	17/H
beige	9/14
besar	17/C
biberón	90/4
biblioteca	83/13
bibliotecario	83/12
bicicleta	76/11
biftec	36/2
bigote	13/10
billetera	55/9
billetes	10/1
bistec	36/2
blanco	9/5
blusa	48/2
boca	60/6

boleto	80/2
bolígrafo	2/10
bolitas de algodón	65/4
bolsa	40/11, 55/5
bolsa de agua caliente	65/7
bolsa de harina	37/6
bombero	74/3
borde	72/10
borrador	2/3
botas	50/7
botella de soda	37/3
botiquín	27/9
botón	57/4
brazo	58/12
brazo roto	63/14
brécol	34/1
brindar	94/B
brócoli	34/1
bufanda	50/10
buzón	71/4
buzones	23/11

C

cabello	13, 60/1
cabello café	13/19
cabello corto	13/12
cabello gris	13/21
cabello lacio	13/14
cabello largo	13/11
cabello negro	13/20
cabello ondulado	13/15
cabello rizo	13/16
cabello rojo	13/18
cabello rubio	13/17
cabeza	58/11, 60
cadera	58/7
caerse	75/A
café	9/10, 38/11
caja	54/1-9
caja de cereal	37/10
caja de herramientas	31/9
caja registradora	40/8
cajera	40/6, 43/12
cajón	26/3
calcetines	51/8
caldero	25/2
calendario	5
cálido	8/10
caliente	8/9
California	98/5
calvo	13/13

calzoncillos	51/2
cama	26/7
camarera	43/7
camarero	43/6
camarones	36/12
cambiar las sábanas	29/L
cambiar pañales	91/B
cambio	55/7
caminar	73/I
camión	76/3
camionero	85/19
camioneta	76/4
camisa	48/4
camiseta	49/7, 51/1
canasta	27/10
canasta de compras	40/3
canasta de lavandería	56/5
(pelo) canoso	13/21
cansado	19/10
cantante	86/14
cantar	17/E
cantidad	70/8
capataz	85/14
capó	77/4
cara	58/1, 60
cargar	41/B
carne de puerco	36/4
carne de res	36/1
carne molida	36/3
carnes	36
carnicería	82/7
carnicero	82/6
Carolina del Norte	99/33
Carolina del Sur	99/40
carpintero	85/16
carrito de bebé	90/2
carrito de compras	40/4
carta	71/5
cartera	55/9
cartero	71/3
cartón de leche	37/1
casarse	21/G
casas y sus alrededores	22
caseta	43/3
casilla	43/3
(pelo) castaño	13/19
catorce	100
cebolla	34/12
ceja	60/4
celebre los días de fiesta	94–95
centavo prieto	10/4
centavos	10/8
Centígrados	102
centímetro	101
cepillarse los dientes	14/D
cepillo	30/8, 61/2
cepillo de dientes	61/4
cerdo	36/4
cereal	38/10
cerebro	59/24
cerezas	35/12
cerradura rota	32/8
cerrajero	84/3
cerrar la ventana	3/I
césped	22/8
cien	100
ciento	100
cierre	57/5
cinco	100
cincuenta	100
cine	69/18
cinta de medir	31/7, 101
cintura	58/6
cinturón	48/6
cinturón de seguridad	77/14
círculo	9/1
ciruelas	35/9
ciudad	78/2, 3
(azul) claro	9/16
clavo	31/15
cliente	40/5
clima	8
clóset	26/1
cobija	26/11
cobrar pasajes	89/V
cocer vegetales al vapor	47/I
cocina	25
cocinar la cena	15/N
cocinero	43/1
cochera	22/6
código postal	71/10
codo	59/17
col	34/2
cola	70/5
colcha	26/10
colgar	57/B
colocar	87/B, E
Colorado	98/6
colores	9
collar	55/4
comer al aire libre	95/J
comer una gran comida	95/Q

comisaría	68/5
cómoda	26/2
comprar víveres	73/G
compresa de hielo	65/5
comprobante de depósito	70/11
comprobante de retiro	70/10
computadora	2/13
comunidad	68-69
con neblina	8/7
conducir un autobús	89/O
conductor de autobús	85/15
congelación	8/13
congelador	25/15
Connecticut	98/7
conseguir un trabajo	20/D
conserje	84/8
construir casas	88/J
construir muebles	88/K
consultorio	83/16
contadora	86/9
contento	18/2
continentes	96
control de seguridad	80/4
contusión	62/9
conversar	3/L
conversión de temperaturas	102
corazón	59/26
corbata	48/5
cordero	36/7
corralito	90/9
corregir	57/D
correr	91/E
corta	53/14
cortadora de césped	31/14
cortadura	62/8
cortar brécol	46/C
cortar brócoli	46/C
cortar carne	88/E
cortar césped	88/F
cortar el bizcocho	17/I
cortar el césped	29/R
cortar el pastel	17/I
cortar pelo	88/D
cortina de baño	27/2
cortinas	24/4, 26/5
coser	57/A
costurera	57/6
crema	38/2, 64/3
crema de afeitar	61/7
cruce de peatones	72/3
cruzando el tráfico	79/7

cruzar la calle	73/E
cuaderno	2/12
cuadrado	9/3
cuarenta	100
cuarto	100, 101
cuarto de dormir	26
cuarto de taza	101
cuarto para las once	7/7
cuatro	100
el 4 de julio	95
cubeta	30/11
cubierto de hielo	8/6
cubiertos	42/2
cucarachas	33/13
cuchara	42/13
cucharada	101
cucharadita	101
cuchillo	42/12
cuello	58/2
cuenta	10/9, 10
cuerpo	58-59
cuidado de la ropa	56-57
cuidar a niños	89/L
cuidar jardines	89/N
cuna	90/10, 12
curita	65/1

CH

chaleco (de plumón)	50/2
chamarra	50/1
champú	61/5
chapa de matrícula	77/1
chaqueta	50/1
chavito prieto	10/4
cheque	70/6
chícharos	34/15
chimenea	22/1
chofer de autobús	85/15
chuleta de puerco	45/18
chupón	90/3

D

Dakota del Norte	99/34
Dakota del Sur	99/41
dar gracias	95/P
dar regalos de San Valentín	94/C
dar un regalo a	17/A
dar vuelta	73/J
darse una ducha	14/C
de Centígrados a Fahrenheit	102
de compras en el supermercado	40-41

de estatura media	12/2
de Fahrenheit a Centígrados	102
de la ciudad	78/3
de peso medio	12/5
debajo de la caja	54/9
décimo	100
decir adiós con la mano	81/C
decorar el árbol	95/T
dedo	58/8
dedo del pie	59/23
dedo del pie infectado	63/16
dejar	91/A
Delaware	98/8
delgado	12/6
demostrar la tarjeta de seguro	67/D
dentista	83/14
dentro de la caja	54/6
Departamento de Registro de Vehículos	69/16
deportes	92
desagüe	27/4
desagüe tapado	33/11
desastres naturales	74–75
desayunarse	15/I
descansar	64/B
describiendo a gente	12–13
describiendo ropa	52–53
desde la ciudad	78/3
desmayarse	63/C
desodorante	61/10
despertarse	14/A
destornillador	31/3
detenerse	73/D
detergente	56/2
detrás de la caja	54/8
día	5/14
Día de Acción de Gracias	95
Día de las Brujas	95
Día de los Enamorados	94
Día de los Soldados Muertos	94
diciembre	4/12
diecinueve	100
dieciocho	100
dieciséis	100
diecisiete	100
diente	60/11
diez	100
diez en punto	7/4
diez y quince	7/5
diez y treinta	7/6
dinero	10
dirección	71/9
dirección del remitente	71/7
dirigir	87/D
disfrazarse	95/M
Distrito de Columbia	99/51
divorciarse	21/H
doblar	56/D
doce	100
dólar	10/2
dolor de cabeza	62/3
dolor de diente	62/6
dolor de espalda	62/4
dolor de estómago	62/5
dolor de garganta	63/12
dolor de muela	62/6
dolor de oído	62/7
dolores	62–63
domingo	5/1
donas	44/9
dormirse	15/P
dos	100
drogas	64/1
drenaje	27/4
ducha	27/1
duraznos	35/10
E	
edad	13
edificio de apartamentos	23
edificio de oficinas	69/17
ejercicio	93
ejotes	34/7
electricista	84/2
emergencias	74–75
empacador	40/12
empacar	41/H
emparedado	44/10
empezar la escuela	20/B
empleada doméstica	84/4
empleado de mantenimiento	85/17
empleado de mudanzas	84/9
empleado postal	71/1
empujar	41/A
en el trabajo	88
en la carretera (Preposiciones II)	78–79
en la tienda (Preposiciones I)	54
en un aeropuerto	80–81
en un consultorio médico	66–67
en un restaurante	43
enamorarse	21/F
encendido	77/11
enero	4/1

enfermarse	21/K
enfermera	66/7
enojado	18/1
ensalada	45/14
entrada	23/5
entrada de automóvil	22/7
entrando a la gasolinera	79/8
entrar	3/D
entrar a la tienda	73/B
entre las cajas	54/4
entusiasmados	18/7
envases	37
envenenarse	75/D
enviar tarjetas	95/R
enviar una carta	73/F
equipaje	80/3
escalera	23/12, 31/10
escalones	23/6
escalones dañados	33/9
escape de incendio	23/3
escoba	30/2
escoger	41/D
escribir	3/A
escribir el nombre en letra de molde	67/B
escribir una receta	67/J
escritorio	2/7
escuchar	3/F
escuchar música	93/L
escuela	68/1
esculpir una calabaza	95/L
espaguetis	45/15
espalda	59/15
espejo	27/8
esperar	67/E
esperar el autobús	73/K
espinaca	34/4
esponja	30/9
esposa	16/10
esposo	16/9
esquina	72/5
estación de autobuses	69/13
estación de bomberos	68/2
estación de policía	68/5
estación de trenes	69/14
estacionamiento	69/15, 21
estaciones del año	4
Estados Unidos de América	98–99
estampilla	71/8
estante	24/12, 40/1
estar parado	3/N
estar sentado	3/M
estatura	12
este	97/17
estéreo	24/13
estilista	82/8
estómago	59/27
estornudar	63/A
estrecharse las manos	81/F
estrellas	6/7
estudiante	2/5
estudiar	15/L
estufa	25/6
Europa	96/3
eventos de la vida	20–21
examinar al paciente	67/F
excavar	87/C
extra grande	53/20
F	
factura	10/10
facturar equipaje	81/A
Fahrenheit	102
falda	48/3
fallecer	21/L
familia	16
farmacéutico	82/1
farmacia	82/2
faros delanteros	77/2
febrero	4/2
fecha	70/7
feliz	18/2
fideos	39/17
fiebre	62/2
fiesta de cumpleaños	17
firma	70/9
firmar el nombre	67/C
flaco	12/6
florería	68/9
Florida	98/9
flotar una bandera	94/G
formas	9
formulario de seguro	66/3
fotógrafo	86/6
frasco de café	37/7
fregadero	25/10
freír cebollas y pimientos	46/F
freno	77/12
frente	60/2
frente a la caja	54/7
fresas	35/11
fresco	8/11
frijoles	39/16

frío	8/12
frutas	35
fuego	74/2
funda	26/9
G	
gabinete	25/12
gafas	55/8
gafas de sol	49/3
galería	69/19
galón	101
galletas	39/21
gancho	57/9
garaje	22/6
gasolinera	82/5
gatear	91/D
gaveta	26/3
gavetero	26/2
gente	11
Georgia	98/10
giro postal	71/12
gis	2/2
gordo	12/4
gorra	48/10, 50/4
gorra de béisbol	49/6
gotas	64/5
gotera	32/1
gotero	64/6
grados	102
graduarse	20/C
gramo	101
grande	12/7, 53/19
granjero	85/20
grifo	27/3
grifo con gotera	33/10
gris	9/11
gruesa	52/1
guantes	50/13
guantes de hule	30/7
una guardería infantil	90–91
guardia de seguridad	70/3
guineos	35/1
H	
habichuelas	39/16
habichuelas tiernas	34/7
hacer arreglos	57/D
hacer ejercicio	64/F
hacer excursión	92/B
hacer la cama	28/A
hacer una llamada telefónica	73/C
hacer una parrillada	95/J
hacia la ciudad	78/2
hambriento	19/11
hamburguesa	44/11
harina	38/13
Hawaii	98/11
helado	45/21
heridas	62–63
hermana	16/4
hermano	16/5
herramientas para el hogar	31
hervir agua	46/B
hija	16/13
hijo	16/12
hilo	57/2
hogar	31
hojas de afeitar	61/9
hombre	11/5
hombre de negocios	86/8
hombro	58/3
hongos	34/14
horas del día	6
hornear un guiso	47/L
hornillo	25/6
horno	25/7
horno microondas	25/1
hoy	5/12
huevos	38/4
huevos estrellados	44/3
huevos fritos	44/3
huevos revueltos	44/1
humo	74/1
huracán	74/13
I	
Idaho	98/12
iglesia	68/6
Illinois	98/13
impermeable	50/8
Indiana	98/14
Indico	96/13
inodoro	27/12
inodoro tapado	32/6
intersección	72/6, 72–73
inundación	74/10
invierno	4/13
inyección	64/4
Iowa	98/15
ir a correr	93/N
ir a esquiar	92/H
ir a nadar	93/M

ir al cine	93/J
ir de campamento	92/A
ir de compras navideñas	95/S
ir en busca de huevos de Pascua	94/F

J

jamón	36/6
jarabe	44/8
jardín	22/13
jardinero	84/5
jeans	49/4
joven	13/22
joyas	55
jubilarse	20/E
jueves	5/5
jugar	91/C
jugar baloncesto	92/E
jugar béisbol	92/G
jugar fútbol	92/F
jugar fútbol americano	92/D
jugar tenis	92/C
jugo	39/20
juguete	90/7
julio	4/7
junio	4/6
junto a la caja	54/3

K

Kansas	98/16
Kentucky	98/17
kilogramo	101
kilómetro	101

L

labio	60/10
lámpara	24/6
langosta	36/11
lápiz	2/11
larga	53/13
lata de sopa	37/8
lavabo	27/7
lavadora	56/1
lavandería automática	56
lavaplatos	43/2
lavar la ropa	29/P
lavar las ventanas	29/N
lavar los platos	28/F
lavarse la cara	14/E
leche	38/1
lechuga	34/3
leer	3/E

lengua	60/12
lentes	55/8
levantar	91/K
levantar la mano	3/K
levantarse	14/B
libra(s)	101
librería	68/8
librero	24/12
libro	2/8
ligera	52/2
limones	35/7
limones verdes	35/8
limpia	52/5
limpiador	30/1, 6
limpiamesas	43/5
limpiar el baño	28/C
limpiar el cuarto	28/B
limpiar el piso	29/O
linterna eléctrica	31/8
litro	101
longitud, altura y distancia	101
lugares de trabajo	82–83
Luisiana	98/18
luna	6/6
lunes	5/2

LL

llanta	77/8
llave	27/3
llave de agua con gotera	33/10
llave de tuerca	31/2
llegar	81/D
llenar el formulario	67/A
llevar	41/B
llorar	91/J
lloviendo	8/1

M

madre	16/3
madura	13/23
maestra	2/4
Maine	98/19
maíz	34/5
maleta	80/3
maletera	77/6
manejar un autobús	89/O
manejar un camión	89/Q
manejar un taxi	89/P
manguera	31/11
mano	58/5
mantelito individual	42/3

mantener piscinas	89/M
mantequilla	38/6
manzanas	35/3
mañana	5/13, 6/1
mapas	96–99
máquina de coser	57/7
margarina	38/7
mariscos	36
martes	5/3
martillar	87/H
martillo	31/4
Maryland	98/20
marzo	4/3
Massachusetts	98/21
mayo	4/5
mayonesa	39/26
mecánico	82/3
mecanógrafo	86/2
mecer	91/H
media taza	101
mediana	53/18
medianoche	7/3
medias	51/6
medicinas	64/1
médico	66/6
medidas	101
medidas líquidas	101
mediodía	7/2
medir	87/G
mejilla	60/8
melancólico	19/14
melocotones	35/10
menear cebollas y pimientos	46/G
mensajero	86/5
mentón	60/7
menú	43/8
mercado de frutas y verduras	83/18
mesa	42/1
mesa de noche	26/14
mesa puesta	42
mesera	43/7
mesero	43/6
meses	4
mesita	24/8
mesita central	24/9
meter	41/E, 56/A
metro	101
mezclar ingredientes	47/K
Michigan	98/22
miércoles	5/4
mil	100

miligramo	101
mililitro	101
milla	101
millón	100
Minesota	98/23
mirar la ropa	73/H
mirar los escaparates	73/H
Misisipí	98/24
Misurí	98/25
mitones	50/12
mochila	50/6
mojado	53/11
moneda de cinco	10/5
moneda de diez	10/6
moneda de veinticinco	10/7
monedas	10/3
Montana	98/26
morado	9/13
morir	21/L
mostaza	39/24
mostrador	25/14
mostrador de pago	40/9
motocicleta	76/5
muchacha	11/2
muchacho	11/3
mudarse	21/J
mujer	11/4
mujer de negocios	86/8
muletas	65/8
mundo	97
muñeca	58/10
muslo	59/16
N	
nacer	20/A
naranjas	35/4
nariz	60/9
nariz sangrienta	63/17
navaja de afeitar	61/8
Navidad	95
Nebraska	99/27
negro	9/4
nervioso	18/4
Nevada	99/28
nevando	8/2
nevera	25/16
nevera descompuesta	33/12
New Hampshire	99/29
niña	11/2, 6
niñera	86/12
niño	11/3, 6

no hay agua caliente	32/7
no hay calefacción	32/5
noche	6/4
Nochevieja	94
noreste	97/19
noroeste	97/20
norte	97/15
Norteamérica	96/4
nostálgico	19/14
noveno	100
noventa	100
noviembre	4/11
nublado	8/5
nueces	35/14
nueva	52/3
Nueva Jersey	99/30
Nueva York	99/32
nueve	100
Nuevo México	99/31
números	100

O

obrero de fábrica	85/13
océanos	96
octavo	100
octubre	4/10
ocupaciones	82–86
ochenta	100
ocho	100
oeste	97/18
oficina de correos	68/4, 71
Ohio	99/35
ojo	60/5
Oklahoma	99/36
olla	25/2
once	100
onzas	101
operador de tren	85/23
operaria de máquina de coser	85/22
ordenar el cuarto	28/B
Oregón	99/37
oreja	60/3
orejeras	50/14
orientaciones	97
(azul) oscuro	9/17
otoño	4/16

P

paciente	66/5
Pacífico Norte	96/9
Pacífico Sur	96/10

padre	16/2
padres	16/11
pagador automático	70/4
pagadora	70/1
pagar	41/C
pala	31/13
palacio de justicia	68/3
pan	38/9
pan tostado	44/4
panadería	68/10
panecillo	44/5
panecillo inglés	44/5
panqueques	44/7
pantaleta	51/4
pantalón corto	49/9
pantalones	48/7
pantimedia	51/5
pantorrilla	59/19
pantuflas	51/12
pañal	90/6
paño para lavarse	61/6
papa	34/11
papa al horno	45/17
papas fritas	44/12
papel	2/9
papel higiénico	27/13
paquete	71/2
paquete de galletas	37/4
paquete de pan	37/5
parabrisas	77/5
parada de autobús	72/11
paraguas	50/9
paramédico	74/6
pared	24/2
pared cuarteada	32/2
parque	68/7
parquímetro	72/8
partes de un automóvil	77
partir	81/B
pasabordo	80/5
pasajero	80/1
Pascua	94
pasillo	23/8, 40/2
pasta	39/17
pasta de dientes	61/3
pastel de manzana	45/22
patio	22/11
patio posterior	22/12
pavo	36/9
peatón	72/2
pecho	58/4

peinarse	14/F
peine	61/1
pelar papas	46/A
pelo	13, 60/1
pelo café	13/19
pelo corto	13/12
pelo gris	13/21
pelo lacio	13/14
pelo largo	13/11
pelo negro	13/20
pelo ondulado	13/15
pelo rizo	13/16
pelo rojo	13/18
pelo rubio	13/17
peluquera	82/8
peluquería	82/11
peluquero	82/10
Pensilvania	99/38
pepino	34/10
pequeña	12/8, 53/17
peras	35/5
perro caliente	44/13
pesado	12/4
pesar	41/G
pesar al paciente	67/G
pescado	36/10
pescador	85/18
peseta	10/7
peso	12
pesos	101
pesos sólidos	101
pezón	90/5
picadura de insecto	62/11
picar pimientos	46/E
pie(s)	59/21, 101
pierna	58/14
pijama	51/10
píldoras	64/2
piloto	80/8
pimienta	39/23
pimiento	34/9
pinta	101
pintar	87/K
pintar huevos de Pascua	94/E
pintor	84/6
pinzas	31/1
piso	23/2, 24/3
piza	45/16
pizarra	2/1
pizarrón	2/1
placa	77/1
plancha	56/7
planchar	56/C
plantar un árbol	29/Q
plátanos	35/1
platillo	42/8
plato	42/5
plato hondo	42/4
plomera	84/1
policía	74/8
pollo	36/8
pollo frito	45/20
poner	41/E, 56/A, 87/B
poner una inyección	67/I
ponerse a dieta	64/G
por debajo de la caja	54/2
por encima de la caja	54/1
porche	22/3
portero	84/11
preocupada	19/9
preparando una comida	46–47
primavera	4/14
primero	5/8, 100
primeros auxilios	65
primos	16/8
probarse	57/C
problemas caseros	32–33
productos lácteos	38–39
programadora	86/4
puerta	80/6
puerta del frente	22/4
puesto de periódicos	72/7
pulgada	101
pulgar	58/9
pulmón	59/25
pulsera	55/2
puré de papas	45/19
Q	
quehaceres domésticos	28–29
quemador	25/4
quemarse	63/D
queso	38/5
quince	100
quinientos	100
quinto	100
quitar	87/A
R	
rallar queso	46/H
ranura	56/4
raspar	87/J

rastrillar las hojas	28/I
rastrillo	31/12
ratones	33/14
rayos equis	66/9
rebanar cebollas	46/D
recepcionista	66/2
receta	66/10
recibir	81/E
recibir flores	94/D
recibo	10/11
recipiente de yogur	37/2
reclamo de equipaje	80/9
recogedor	30/3
recoger	91/K
recoger basura	89/U
recoger boletos	89/W
refresco	39/19
refrigerador	25/16
refrigerador descompuesto	33/12
regar las plantas	28/H
regla	101
regresar a casa	15/M
regreso de botellas	40/13
reír	17/B
reloj	7, 7/1, 55/6
reloj despertador	26/13
reparar aparatos domésticos	88/A
reparar automóviles	88/B
reparar plomería	88/C
reparar teles	88/A
repartidor	83/20
repartir correo	89/R
repartir paquetes	89/T
repartir víveres	89/S
repollo	34/2
reportera	86/7
resfriado	62/1
retirarse	20/E
reunirse con familia y amigos	95/O
Rhode Island	99/39
robo	74/7
robo con violencia	74/9
rodilla	59/18
rojo	9/6
rollo de papel higiénico	37/9
ropa básica	48
ropa informal	49
ropa interior y de dormir	51
ropa para clima frío	50
rosado	9/15
rutinas diarias	14–15

S	
sábado	5/7
sábanas	26/12
sacar	41/F, 56/B
sacar la basura	28/J
sacar una fotografía	17/G
sacudir los muebles	28/E
sal	39/22
sala	24
sala de espera	66/1
sala de reconocimiento	66/8
salchicha	44/2
salero y pimentero	42/9
salida	80/6
salida (de incendio)	23/4
saliendo de la gasolinera	79/9
salir	3/C, 81/B
salir de casa	15/J
salir de la tienda	73/A
salir por obsequios o travesuras	95/N
salón de belleza	82/9
salón de clase de inglés	2–3
salsa de tomate	39/25
saludarse	81/F
sandalias	49/5
sandías	35/13
sarpullido	62/10
sartén	25/5
sastre	57/8
secadora	56/3
secar los platos	28/G
sección de fumar	43/10
sección de no fumar	43/11
seco	53/12
secretaria	86/1
sediento	19/12
segundo	5/9, 100
seis	100
seiscientos veintiuno	100
sello postal	71/8
semáforo	72/1
semana	5/15
sencillo	10/6
seno	58/13
sentimientos	18–19
señalar	3/B
septiembre	4/9
séptimo	100
ser enyesado	64/E
servilleta	42/10
serrucho	31/5

sesenta	100
setenta	100
sexto	100
siete	100
silla	2/6
silla alta	43/9
silla de ruedas	65/10
sillón	24/5
sistema de intercomunicación	23/13
sobre	71/6
sobre la caja	54/5
sobre la carretera	78/1
sobrina	16/14
sobrino	16/15
soda	39/19
sofá	24/11
sofocarse	75/E
sol	6/5
soldado	85/21
soleado	8/4
sonajero	90/11
sonreír	17/D
sopa	39/18
soplar las velitas	17/F
sorprendida	19/8
sostén	51/7
sótano	23/7
sótano inundado	33/15
subiendo la colina	79/6
subir	87/I
sucia	52/6
sudadera	49/10, 50/5
suelta	53/16
suéter	50/3
superintendente	84/10
supermercado	40-41, 68/11
supervisar	87/D
sur	97/16
Suramérica	96/5
sureste	97/21
suroeste	97/22

T

tabla de planchar	56/6
tablero	77/9
taladro	31/6
talón	59/22
tamaño	12
tanque de gasolina	77/7
tapete	24/10
tarde	6/2

tarjeta de crédito	10/12
tarjeta de embarque	80/5
tarjeta de identificación	55/10
tarjeta de seguro	66/4
tarjeta postal	71/11
taxi	76/6
taxista	84/12
taza	42/7, 101
tazón	42/4
té	38/12
techo	22/2, 24/1
techo cuarteado	32/4
tele	24/14, 88/A
teléfono	24/7
teléfono público	72/4
televisión	24/14
temblor	74/11
temperatura	8/8
tenedor	42/11
tener puntos	64/C
tener un ataque al corazón	75/B
tener un bebé	21/I
tener una operación	64/A
Tenesí	99/42
tercero	5/10, 100
tercio de taza	101
termómetro	65/3
terremoto	74/11
tetera	25/3
tetilla	90/5
Texas	99/43
tía	16/7
tiempo	4-7
tiempo libre	92-93
tienda por departamentos	69/20
tijeras	57/3
tina	27/5
tintorero	57
tío	16/6
tiza	2/2
toalla	27/11
toalla calentadora	65/6
toallas de papel	30/10
tobillo	59/20
tobillo hinchado	63/15
tocar un instrumento	93/I
tocino	36/5
toma de corriente	30/12
tomar en los brazos	91/I
tomar la temperatura	67/H
tomar medicina	64/D

Index

Indice

tomar una siesta	91/G		vegetales	34
tomate	34/8		veinte	100
tornado	74/12		veintiuno	100
tornillo	31/16		vellón	10/5
toronjas	35/6		vendaje	65/2
toser	63/B		vendedor	86/11
tostadora	25/13		vender periódicos	88/I
trabajador de construcción	84/7		vender ropa	88/G
trabajador de limpieza pública	83/19		vender verduras	88/H
trabajadora de guardería infantil	90/I		ventana	22/5
trabajar	15/K		ventana de servicio rápido	70/2
trabajar con la computadora	3/G		ventana rota	32/3
traer	91/A		ventoso	8/3
traje	48/9		ver fuegos artificiales	95/K
traje de baño (de hombre)	49/1		ver la pantalla	3/H
traje de baño (de mujer)	49/2		ver televisión	93/K
traje de entrenamiento	49/10		ver un desfile	94/H
transacciones bancarias	70		verano	4/15
transporte	76		verde	9/9
trapeador	30/I		Vermont	99/45
trapear el piso	29/O		vestíbulo	23/9
trapo	30/5		vestido	48/I
tratamientos	64		vestir	91/L
trece	100		vestirse	14/H
treinta	100		vieja	52/4
tren	76/9		viernes	5/6
tren subterráneo	76/7		Virginia	99/46
tres	100		Virginia Occidental	99/48
triángulo	9/2		visitar un cementerio	94/I
triste	18/3		víveres	40/10
trusa	51/3		volante	77/10
tubo de pasta dental	37/12			
			W	
U			wafles	44/6
ungüento	64/3		Washington	99/47
uniforme	48/11		Wisconsin	99/49
uno	100		Wyoming	99/50
Utah	99/44			
utensilios de limpieza	30		**Y**	
uvas	35/2		yarda(s)	101
			yogur	38/8
V				
vaciar	87/F		**Z**	
vaciar el basurero	29/K		zanahoria	34/13
vaciar leche	47/J		zapato	48/8
vara de una yarda	101		zapatos de tenis	49/8
vaso	42/6			